GLASGOW ON A PLATE 2

First published 2000
by Black and White Publishing Ltd, Edinburgh
ISBN 1 902927 12 5
Foreword © Eddie Friel, 2000
Introduction © Ferrier Richardson, 2000
Text and Recipes © The Contributors, 2000
Photographs © Alan Donaldson, 2000

British Library Cataloguing in Publication Data:
A catalogue record for this book is available
from the British Library.

Printed and bound in Spain by Bookprint, S.L, Barcelona

GLASGOW ON A PLATE 2

EDITED BY

FERRIER RICHARDSON

PHOTOGRAPHS BY **ALAN DONALDSON**

BW

CONTENTS

INTRODUCTION

I am absolutely delighted to be writing this introduction to *Glasgow on a Plate* 2.

Thanks to the enormous success of the first edition we were inundated with requests for another volume.

We have included a few restaurants from the first book and invited some more of Glasgow's favourite dining spots to join us in this venture. Once again we have a great collection of recipes using a variety of Scottish and international produce and Alan Donaldson has captured some fantastic images with his magnificent photography.

People have been using the book as a guide to sourcing out the best restaurants in the city and some readers have became obsessed with getting every chapter signed by the relevant chef!

Once again can I thank Mr Eddie Friel and the Glasgow Tourist Board for all the support. I have been particularly pleased that they feel that the book is a great asset to them when it comes to selling Glasgow.

I hope you enjoy our second edition as much as I have enjoyed putting it together. With the amount of new restaurants opening who is to say there won't be a third.

Ferrier.

FOREWORD

This second helping of *Glasgow on a Plate* contains even more mouth watering recipes prepared by Glasgow's chefs and edited by world renowned chef Ferrier Richardson – whose passion for food is equalled only by his ardour for Glasgow. His credentials as a chef of international stature are well documented. As past manager of both the Scottish and British Culinary Olympic Teams, Ferrier led his colleagues to win the Top Team award (1993), as well as a clutch of gold and sliver medals.

Voted 'Top regional UK City' for the choice and quality of its restaurants in *Harden's Top UK Restaurants 1999* guide and recently described in the US magazine *Travel & Leisure* as: 'The United Kingdom's Hippest and Most Happening City', Glasgow offers all the buzz and excitement you would expect from one of Europe's liveliest destinations – making it the perfect place for a cultural or gastronomic short break.

In keeping with Glasgow's innate sense of style and highly developed fashion flair, the architectural and design features of the city's eateries are viewed as importantly as the quality of cooking and freshness of ingredients. From art deco oyster bars and *fin-de-siècle* brasseries, to art nouveau tearooms and the very latest in minimalist, millennium chic, Glasgow's restaurants cover the complete style and taste spectrum.

Whatever the surroundings however, the emphasis is always on quality and using fresh local produce including organic vegetables, Scotch lamb, salmon and venison – perhaps washed down with a dram of malt whisky. Glasgow's café-society also gives it a strong European feel and some of the best latte, mocha and espresso are served up with a well-loved, local speciality – caramel shortcake (calorific but worth it!). If world cuisine is on your agenda, you can also dine in a different country every day from Japanese sushi, Pacific Rim and French country cooking, to Indian balti, fresh Italian pasta and of course traditional Scottish fare.

I hope I have whetted your appetite and that you will enjoy not only reading the anecdotes from the city's growing band of outstanding chefs, but also trying out some of their imaginative recipes to bring a flavour of Glasgow to your own dinner parties.

Eddie Friel

We have reproduced recipes as supplied by the chefs,
according to their own individual cooking style.
All recipes serve four, unless otherwise stated.

DAVID CLUNAS

PAPINGO

'This job is a way of life . . . you've got to get a real buzz out of it.'

For as long as I can remember I have been interested in food and cooking. All the time at school there was never any doubt in my mind that I would pursue a career in catering, so as soon as I could leave, I went to Glasgow College of Food Technology. I left there two years later with an HND and a job as a commis chef at the Buttery where I worked for a year under the head chef, Brian Graham. He was an inspiring boss, helping to nurture my interest in cooking into a passion.

By the age of twenty-one I was head chef at a country house hotel in Biggar, which boosted my self-confidence. I learned and developed a lot of skills in that job. Then I returned to Glasgow, to work at the Rogano, where I moved on to senior sous chef. As Rogano is one of Glasgow's most renowned restaurants, I found that working under pressure became part of the daily routine of life. Hard work, but good experience.

After six years there, I was offered and took the job of head chef at Papingo. The pressure is still there, but in a different way. I believe that to get the best out of my staff, and ultimately to produce food to the highest standards – as our customers expect – encouragement and constructive criticism achieve the best results. I suppose I must be doing something right: Papingo has recently been awarded two AA Rosettes.

For me, being a chef lies somewhere between being a tradesman and an artist. You have to know the trade inside out, and be prepared to work on a sort of conveyor belt, all the time trying to inject artistic flair into the whole process: the amalgamation of flavours and presentation of food.

This job is a way of life – you should never become a chef just to pick up a wage packet at the end of the week, you've got to get a real buzz out of it.

SMOKED HADDOCK, SWEET POTATO AND SAFFRON SOUP
WITH CHIVE CRÈME FRAICHE

50g butter

2 medium leeks, finely chopped

3 medium sweet potatoes, peeled, and
    cut into 1cm cubes

275g smoked haddock

1.15 litres fish stock

3 tbsp plain flour

1g pinch of saffron threads

2 tbsp snipped chives

125g crème fraiche

Salt and pepper to taste

Melt butter over a low heat in a thick-bottomed pan.

Add chopped leeks and cubed potatoes to melted butter and sweat in the pan until leeks are tender.

In another pan, gently poach smoked haddock in fish stock for 5 minutes, then remove haddock and flake.

Add the flour to the pan of leek and potato and cook slowly on a low heat for 3-5 minutes (to make a roux). Gradually ladle in fish stock, stirring continuously.

Once all the fish stock is transferred to pan, add in flaked smoked haddock and saffron, then simmer for 25-30 minutes.

Mix snipped chives with crème fraîche and season.

Season soup to taste.

To serve, pour into warm bowls with a dollop of crème fraiche in centre.

ROAST BREAST OF DUCK

WITH PUY LENTILS, SHERRY VINEGAR JUS AND
CARAMELISED SHALLOTS

1 tbsp olive oil

2 red onions, finely diced

125g Puy lentils

500ml chicken stock

1 carrot, finely diced

salt and pepper

4 x 250g duck breasts

12 large shallots, peeled

1 tbsp sugar

For the sauce:

200ml game stock, well reduced

50g redcurrant jelly

50ml sherry vinegar

Heat oil in a saucepan, add red onions and cook until golden brown. Add lentils and sweat off for 2 minutes. Pour in chicken stock and simmer until lentils are tender.

Add carrot just before lentils are ready; by this time all the liquid should have evaporated.

Season to taste and keep warm.

Fry duck skin down on a moderate heat for 15 minutes. This will melt the skin fat, until skin becomes crispy. Turn and cook the other side for up to 5 minutes, ensuring duck is still pink in the middle. Keep warm.

Fry off shallots in a little of the duck fat until golden brown. Put on an ovenproof tray and sprinkle with sugar. Place in a hot oven, 220°C (gas mark 7), for about 5 minutes until shallots soften.

For the sauce: bring game stock and redcurrant jelly to the boil and reduce until it coats the back of a spoon. Add sherry vinegar and season.

To serve, place Puy lentils in the centre of each plate, slice the duck and fan out over the lentils, garnish with caramelised shallots and spoon sauce around.

Photograph on page 3.

CRISP FRIED FILLET OF SALMON

ON A BED OF PEPPERED BOK CHOI WITH AN
ORANGE AND CORIANDER FISH CREAM

olive oil

4 x 225g fillets of salmon (skin left on,
  scales removed)

250g washed and picked bok choi
  leaves

course ground pepper from peppermill

For the sauce:

250ml good-quality fish stock

2 glasses Chablis

grated zest and juice of 4 oranges

500ml double cream

3 tbsp chopped coriander

salt and pepper

Put some olive oil in a heavy-based frying pan; fry salmon, skin-side-down, for 5 minutes on a medium heat or until skin turns crispy.

Turn salmon and cook for a further 2 minutes; ensure salmon is cooked through but still slightly pink in the middle. Leave aside and keep warm.

For the sauce: put fish stock and wine in a pan and reduce until almost evaporated.

Add in orange juice and zest, reduce further until 2 tablespoons are left.

Add the cream, bring to the boil and reduce to a thick creamy consistency.

Add chopped coriander and season to taste.

Sauté bok choi in a wok or frying pan, on a high heat, until just wilted.

Add lots of freshly milled pepper.

To serve, place a bed of bok choi in the centre of each plate, put salmon on top and pour sauce around.

CHOCOLATE AND PISTACHIO TART

325ml double cream

25g castor sugar

115g butter, at room temperature, cut
  into 1cm cubes

400g plain chocolate, chopped into
  small cubes

75ml milk

50g finely chopped, not ground,
  pistachio nuts

Cocoa powder, to dust

100g Mascarpone, sweetened

For the pastry:

125g unsalted butter, cold, cut into
  1cm cubes

75g castor sugar

250g plain flour

pinch of salt

1 small egg

For the pastry: blend butter and castor sugar together. Rub in flour and salt until the mixture resembles fine breadcrumbs. Add egg to bind. Add water, if required. Allow to rest for half an hour.

Roll pastry into 30cm flan ring, and allow to rest again for half an hour. Bake blind at 180°C (gas mark 4) for 15-20 minutes, until golden brown. Leave to cool.

Put cream and sugar in pan and bring to the boil. Pour into a bowl and slowly whisk in butter and chocolate cubes.

Cool mixture a little and stir in cold milk until shiny. Once mixture stiffens slightly, stir in pistachio nuts.

Scrape mixture into cool pastry shell, dust with cocoa powder and refrigerate.

Serve each portion of tart at room temperature with a spoonful of Mascarpone.

Photograph on page 7.

PASCAL ECK

CORINTHIAN

'The ethos of the restaurant is to create simple no-nonsense dishes from carefully sourced, quality produce.'

I became a chef thanks to my grandmother. When we were children, my sisters and I would visit her house every Wednesday (traditionally a mid-week holiday from school in France). She would show me how to prepare and cook fresh produce for all the family. I was captivated by the processes involved and from that moment decided to be a chef. Before long, I was the one cooking meals for everyone, including my grandmother!

I started as an apprentice chef in 1984, aged fifteen, and twice won the silver award for 'Apprentice of the Year' at the college I attended – CFA Saumur. I graduated in classical cuisine in 1984.

My first job was at Les Années Trente in Chinon, France. The restaurant specialised in seafood, and I became head chef when I was nineteen. I then was called for my military service (which is compulsory in France), where I became personal chef to the colonel, catering for his private parties. After ten months I returned to Les Années Trente.

I came to Glasgow to follow my wife, who is Scottish. I met her in Saumur when she was travelling through France. We travelled around Europe for a while, but then decided to settle in Glasgow. We now have a daughter, Emma. I became head chef at Corinthian in December 1999.

Corinthian serves cosmopolitan, modern European cuisine. The ethos of the restaurant is to create simple no-nonsense dishes from carefully sourced, quality produce. We want diners to treat Corinthian as a comfortable and affordable everyday luxury. Great food, at an affordable price.

I have chosen recipes from Corinthian's summer menu. These dishes are always popular with customers; in fact, they're still on the menu, due to popular demand. Obviously, the seafood bouillabaisse is one of my personal favourites and dates back to the experience of my first kitchen, using fresh fish in France. I'm inspired by the sea, sun, seafood and fresh produce.

One last piece of advice for future chefs: cooking is logical, so think everything through before you begin.

PEPPER FRITTERS

2 tbsp olive oil

250g mixed peppers, deseeded and cut
  into strips

$1/2$ small onion, cut into small slices

1 clove of garlic, finely chopped

2 tbsp red wine

1 tbsp balsamic vinegar

$1/2$ tbsp basil, finely chopped

$1/2$ tbsp oregano, finely chopped

Salt and pepper

4 eggs, separated

25g flour

75g grated Parmesan

Mascarpone, to serve

Rich tomato sauce:

$1/2$ onion (finely chopped)

4 shallots (finely sliced)

1 carrot (finely chopped)

2 cloves garlic (finely sliced)

20g basil

225g plum tomatoes

1 tbsp vegetable oil

salt and pepper

Heat 1 tablespoon of olive oil in a pan and add peppers, onion and garlic.

Cook for 2-3 minutes slowly, without colouring the vegetables.

Add red wine, balsamic vinegar, basil and oregano, salt and pepper.

Stew the mix for 2 more minutes on high heat and remove the pan from the stove.

Stir pepper mixture into the egg yolks and add flour.

Whisk egg whites until they form soft peaks.

Fold half the egg whites into the mixture, sprinkle on Parmesan and fold into the
remaining whites.

Heat 1 tablespoon of olive oil in a thick-bottomed frying pan and use a spoon or
ladle to form 1.5cm fritters.

Carefully turn the fritters when they are brown and sufficiently cooked through.

For the tomato sauce: Sweat the onion, shallot, garlic and carrot in the vegetable
oil, add the plum tomatoes and the basil. Cook for 12-15 minutes, blitz and pass
through a medium strainer and season to taste.

Serve stacked on a rich tomato sauce with a dollop of Mascarpone.

Photograph on page 11.

MARINATED CHICKEN BREAST

WITH TABBOULEH & TZATZIKI

4 boneless chicken breasts (corn-fed if
possible, with skin on)

For the marinade:

2 cloves of garlic

1 red chilli

zest and juice of 1 lemon

1 tbsp of olive oil

1 sprig of rosemary

ground pepper

1 tsp spring fresh mint, coarsely
chopped

juice of $1/2$ lemon

2 tomatoes, chopped and deseeded

2 tbsp red onion (finely chopped)

salt and pepper

For the tabbouleh:

100g bulgar wheat

1 tbsp olive oil

1 large sprig of flat-leaf parsley,
coarsely chopped

For the tzatziki:

1 cucumber

3 tbsp Greek yogurt

1 tsp chopped fresh mint

1 clove of garlic (crushed)

salt and fresh ground pepper

First marinade the chicken breasts. Cut the garlic and chilli into large slices. Place all
the marinade ingredients into a bowl and add the chicken. Rub the marinade into the
chicken and refrigerate. Marinade for at least 4 hours but 24 hours is better.

For the tabbouleh: bring a large pan of salted water to a rolling boil. Sprinkle the
bulgar wheat into the water and cook for 5 minutes. Drain and add olive oil and let the
wheat cool. Once cool, add the other ingredients of the tabbouleh and taste for
seasoning.

Heat the grill and place the chickens breasts under. Let them colour before turning.
They should take about 5 minutes. While the chickens are cooking make the tzatziki.

For the tzatziki: halve cucumber lengthways and deseed with a teaspoon. Slice
thinly and place in a bowl. Add the other tzatziki ingredients and chill for serving.

Serve chicken on a bed of tabbouleh with sautéed courgettes or green salad and a
wedge of lemon.

THAI SEAFOOD BOUILLABAISSE

1 monkfish tail, approx 400g

12 raw tiger prawns with heads on

8 king scallops

500g fresh mussels, debearded and
   washed

2 tbsp olive oil

1 small onion, peeled and roughly
   chopped

1/2 bulb of fennel, roughly chopped

1 large carrot, peeled and roughly
   chopped

3cm stick of ginger, peeled and roughly
   chopped

3 stalks of lemon grass, chopped

2 cloves of garlic, chopped

2 red chillies, chopped

zest of 1 lime

1 glass of white wine

1 tin of peeled plum tomatoes

1 tin of coconut milk

Jasmine rice

1 sprig of fresh coriander

Fillet monkfish and cut into 1.5cm dice; keep any trimmings and bones aside. Peel prawns and keep shell and heads aside. Remove the roe and tough muscle from the scallops and keep aside. Refrigerate all the fish.

Heat 1 tablespoon of oil gently in a pan and add the carrot, fennel, onion, lemon grass, garlic and chillies. After 4-5 minutes of gently sweating, add the lime zest. Add the bones and trimmings from the monkfish tails and stir gently.

Meanwhile, place the shells and the heads of the prawns in a small pot and gently crush with the end of a heavy rolling pin, being careful of 'shrapnel'. When the pieces are approximately 1cm in size, add them to the pot with the vegetables and monkfish trimmings. Add wine and boil until almost fully evaporated. Add the tomatoes and coconut milk and simmer very gently for 30 minutes. Blend the sauce in a liquidiser until smooth and pass through a fine sieve, pressing down on the sediment to extract all the flavours. Place the finished sauce in a pan and keep on the simmer.

Bring a large frying pan to high heat with the rest of the oil and first add monkfish. Once monkfish is coloured on one side turn, add scallops and prawns.

Add mussels to the sauce; they should open after 1 minute (if not, discard).

After the fish has been pan-fried, place it on a kitchen towel so that any oil or sediment from the fish is absorbed (to make the final dish cleaner).

Spoon over the sauce and serve with jasmine rice and chopped coriander.

GRATIN OF PINK GRAPEFRUIT AND ORANGE

3 pink grapefruits
5 navel oranges

For the grenadine sabayon:

5 egg yolks
150g castor sugar
250ml or 1 glass dessert wine
1 tbsp grenadine syrup

Prepare fruit first as sabayon must be used immediately.

Peel fruit with a serrated knife and cut the segments out. Arrange them on four plates, alternating the colours.

Heat the grill on the highest heat.

For the sabayon: add all the sabayon ingredients to a bowl wide enough to sit over a pan of simmering water. Whisk over the water until sabayon is thick and fluffy (approximately 5 minutes).

Spoon sauce over fruit and place one at a time under the grill.

Colour slightly and serve with a fruit sorbet.

ANDREW FAIRLIE

ONE DEVONSHIRE GARDENS

'One Devonshire has grown in size and reputation; the food is perhaps simpler than I cooked six years ago.'

I think the fact that I'm still here after six years has surprised a lot of people; it's a long time in a chef's life. The first couple of years were a learning process for me: my first real job under the spotlight. I spent that time organising things the way I wanted and getting a team that I trusted. We decided right at the beginning that there was no point in bringing in really experienced staff. I needed two good strong sous chefs, and once that was sorted we decided to take on youngsters either from college or apprenticeship schemes.

A lot of young people may have a glamorous perception of the industry, but the realities of starting in a kitchen at 'ground level' can prove quite a culture shock. Chefs can spend all their time moaning about the lack of staff, but I think that they need to take some responsibility themselves and go out and recruit properly. The first four to six years are a crucial time for a young chef. Once trainees are in the kitchen, it's very important that time is devoted to training and motivating them; if they manage to get through that first six months to a year, then generally they are fine. I still think that the biggest mistake was doing away with the classical four-year apprenticeship: it killed a massive part of our skill base.

Training is hard work, but you get out what you put in. The majority of staff here have been with me for a while. Some of the young guys have been here for three years, but I tell them to move on. We try to help them do that; for instance, we place people with Michel Roux at the Waterside Inn – the only three-star Michelin restaurant in the country. One Devonshire has grown in size and reputation; the food is perhaps simpler than I cooked six years ago. I would like to see things develop further; I think we are in a very strong position to do that, although we can never rest on our laurels.

LOBSTER
WITH GINGER AND VEGETABLE PEARLS

For the vegetable stock:

1 carrot, peeled and
 diced

1 onion, peeled and
 diced

1 stick celery, diced

30g ginger, diced

1 sprig of thyme

1 sprig of tarragon

6 crushed white
 peppercorns

1 star anise

zest of 1 orange

125ml white wine

1.2 litres cold water

pinch of dried fennel
 seeds

sea salt to taste

2 lobsters (700-900g
 each)

1 small carrot, peeled

½ cucumber, peeled

1 small celeriac

6 large button
 mushrooms

75g shelled peas or
 broad beans

zest of 1 lemon, cut into
 julienne

1 shallot, cut into rings

15g fresh ginger, cut into
 julienne

juice of ½ lemon

100ml double cream

30g unsalted butter

salt and pepper

1 bunch of chives, finely
 chopped, to garnish

a few sprigs of chervil, to
 garnish

For the vegetable stock: put all the vegetable stock ingredients into a saucepan, bring to the boil and simmer for 45 minutes, leave to go cold and then strain.

Bring a large pan of water to the boil and season generously with sea salt. Plunge lobsters into the boiling water and cook for 8-10 minutes. Refresh them under cold running water until thoroughly chilled.

Cut carrot, cucumber, celeriac and mushroom caps with a 0.6cm melon baller. Cook these and the peas individually in boiling salted water and then plunge into iced water. Blanch lemon zest and shallot rings and mix together with drained vegetable pearls.

Remove all meat from lobsters, cut tail into 4 or 6 equal-sized pieces and keep claws whole.

Bring 500ml of vegetable stock to the boil and add ginger and lemon juice, cook for 1 minute, add cream and bring to a rapid boil. Add cooked vegetables and lobster meat, heat gently, then add butter and check seasoning. Divide between four shallow soup plates and garnish with chives and chervil.

POT-ROASTED PHEASANT
WITH BRAISED CHICORY

8 heads of chicory

3 litres water

4 tsp sugar

juice of 1 lemon

170g plain flour

6 egg whites

2 sprigs of thyme

2 female pheasants (450-700g each with giblets removed)

salt and pepper

100g unsalted butter

2 carrots, peeled and diced

2 onions, peeled and diced

6 cloves of garlic

1 egg yolk mixed with 1 tbsp of water (egg yolk glaze)

Trim any wilted or brown leaves from chicory and trim the base. In a saucepan bring 2 litres of cold water, sugar and lemon juice to a simmer, add chicory and simmer gently for 30 minutes until tender. Remove chicory and lay flat until needed.

Put flour into a bowl, add egg whites and mix until dough is soft and pliable; if it is too stiff, add a little water. Wrap in clingfilm and leave at room temperature until needed.

Preheat the oven to 250ºC. Place a sprig of thyme in the cavity of each pheasant with plenty of salt and pepper, then tie birds and season on the outside. In a pan melt butter until foaming, place pheasants on their sides and brown for 3 minutes. Turn and brown on the other side for 3 more minutes, then turn on to their backs for a further 3 minutes. Surround birds with the diced carrots and onions and garlic, turn on to their sides and place in the oven for 5 minutes. Turn on to their other sides for another 5 minutes.

Remove pan from the oven, transfer birds on to a plate and return pan to a high heat for 3-4 minutes until vegetables are browned. Strain off any fat that remains and then add 700ml water to vegetables, scraping off any residue from the bottom of the pan. Cook for 5 minutes and then strain the liquid, squeezing out all the juices from vegetables. You should have at least 250ml. Wash and dry the pan.

Reduce the oven temperature to 220ºC. Squeeze all the water out of the chicory and place in the bottom of the pan. Place pheasants on top and pour over the cooking juices. Roll sealing pastry into a long thick rope, put lid on the pan and seal with pastry. Brush pastry with egg yolk glaze. Place pan in centre of oven for approximately 15 minutes per 450g of pheasant. Remove pan from oven, but do not break seal. Leave to rest for 10-15 minutes. Break seal, remove lid and lift out pheasants. Arrange chicory on a serving plate, carve pheasants, place on top of chicory and strain cooking juices over the top. Serve with a creamy dauphinoise potato and tossed winter salad.

Photograph on page 19.

ANDREW FAIRLIE

GRILLED FILLET OF HALIBUT
WITH ROASTED GARLIC AND LEMON RISOTTO, CONFIT OF
FENNEL AND BLACK OLIVE AND ANCHOVY DRESSING

For the risotto:

1 head of garlic

olive oil

sea salt and pepper

juice and finely grated
   zest of 2 lemons

1 chopped shallot

300g arborio rice

600ml hot fish stock

50ml double cream

For the fennel confit:

6 heads of fennel

juice of 1 lemon

4 star anise

2 litres good olive oil

sea salt

For the tomato confit:

6 vine tomatoes

sea salt

olive oil from fennel confit

**For the black olive and
anchovy dressing:**

16 good-quality black
   olives

1 anchovy fillet

juice of $1/4$ lemon

75ml oil from fennel confit

4 x 200g halibut fillets

28 capers, deep-fried

For the risotto: cut off the top 0.6cm of the garlic head. Drizzle with olive oil and sea salt, wrap in tin foil and roast in a medium oven for 25-30 minutes. Open foil during the last 10 minutes of cooking to colour slightly. Squeeze garlic pulp from each clove and purée with juice from 1 lemon. Heat a little olive oil and sweat shallot, add rice and cook for 2-3 minutes, add garlic purée and lemon zest, add half the fish stock and simmer till absorbed. Add the rest of the stock little by little till the rice is cooked *al dente*, then add rest of lemon juice, double cream, and season to taste.

For the fennel confit: remove tough outer leaves from fennel bulbs and place into deep saucepan. Cut lemon in half and squeeze juice over fennel, add star anise and cover with olive oil. Season with sea salt. Cover with greaseproof paper and slowly bring oil to just below simmering point. Cook fennel very slowly (preferably over a pilot light) for 4 hours or until very soft. Remove fennel bulbs and cut into quarters. Save fennel oil for tomato confit, and black olive and anchovy dressing.

For the tomato confit: blanch tomatoes, quarter and deseed. Lay the tomato petals on to a wire rack and sprinkle with sea salt. Dry overnight in a warm oven. Place tomato petals into a shallow saucepan, cover with olive oil from fennel recipe and heat very gently for 20 minutes. Leave to cool.

For the black olive and anchovy dressing: stone olives, chop anchovy and add lemon juice and olive oil. Blitz all ingredients together for 1 minute. Leave to settle for 1 hour and mix gently just before serving.

To serve, brush halibut with olive oil, season and grill on a very hot chargrill until cooked: 3-4 minutes. Heat fennel quarters and tomato petals in olive oil. Spoon risotto on to centre of a large plate, and arrange fennel and tomatoes around risotto. Spoon black olive oil dressing around vegetables, place halibut on to risotto and garnish with deep-fried capers.

CARAMELISED PEAR, HONEY AND ALMOND TART

(Serves 6)

300g sweet pastry
700g pears
100g honey
30g flaked almonds
icing sugar
crème fraiche, to serve

For the Sweet Pastry:
250g flour
100g butter, diced

100g icing sugar
pinch salt
2 eggs

For the batter:
2 eggs
2 egg yolks
80g sugar
20g cornflour
225ml whipping cream

For the sweet pastry: sift flour on to work surface. Add butter, work with fingertips until soft. Add icing sugar and salt. Add eggs. Knead 2-3 times until the paste comes together. Wrap in clingfilm for an hour to rest before rolling out.

Preheat oven to 180°C (gas mark 4).

Line a 26cm flan ring with sweet pastry and rest in the fridge for 30 minutes. Line flan ring with greaseproof paper and baking beans and bake for 10 minutes.

Peel, quarter and core the pears. Cut each quarter into 4 again lengthways.

Heat a non-stick pan with the honey until honey foams and begins to colour slightly. Add pears and continue to cook over a fast heat for 5-7 minutes, until pears begin to caramelise. Remove from the heat and drain on to a cooking rack.

For the batter: whisk eggs, egg yolks and sugar until doubled in volume, fold in the cornflour, then add whipping cream and mix well.

Arrange pears in the pre-cooked flan ring, pour in half of the batter, just enough to cover the pears. Put back into oven for 5 minutes, then pour remaining batter over and sprinkle flaked almonds on top.

Return to oven for another 15 minutes. Remove from the oven. The tart will have large bubbles on the surface; just leave them – they will disappear as the tart begins to cool.

Sprinkle tart with icing sugar and eat warm or at room temperature with crème fraiche.

DONALD FLANAGAN

CAFÉ MAO

'Every single dish we do is cooked to order. It's all fresh, and we use mainly Scottish produce'

We first opened Mao in Dublin in 1997. Halfway

through 1998 we were looking for new sites and Glasgow came up. We were one of the first of the new restaurants to come down to Merchant City; we're glad to see that it's growing and we're excited by the new development that's currently underway. The reaction in Glasgow has been great. We wondered how the food would go down, but we've been delighted with how it's taken off.

We've just opened a second Mao in Ireland in Dun Laoghaire and that's been absolutely flying from the word go. It's really taken us by surprise.

The idea for the food for Mao stemmed in part from the fact that I had travelled extensively in Asia and Australia; I found out a lot about the food and really liked it. Then I went to London and worked with a Vietnamese chef, Mai Ngoc Henry who knew all the Asian cuisines; she taught me a lot. I went back to Dublin, met with the other three directors – Ronnie Reilly, Graham Campbell and Rosie Campbell – and the time seemed right to open Mao: right time, right food, right place.

Every single dish we do is cooked to order. It's all fresh, and we use mainly Scottish produce – apart from a few of the Asian herbs and spices. We also have open-plan kitchens, which I think is reassuring for a lot of people.

We try to change the menu three times a year, but it takes a lot of effort and thought to do the food authentically. Sourcing the ingredients is another big issue; for example we have to buy the Thai basil from Thailand as no one has successfully grown it in Europe.

We have an extremely regular clientele, but there are no boundaries to it; we didn't set out for a target market. There's always a good mix of businessmen, kids, housewives; it's for everybody.

With the two restaurants in Ireland, and the one here in Glasgow all on the go, we will take a bit of a rest before rushing on; then we'll move forward from there. We have put an awful lot of work into this. It's tiring, but we're generally very happy.

THAI RARE BEEF SALAD

2 x 200g sirloin steaks, trimmed

1 head butter-leaf lettuce

1 cup mixed fresh herbs, coriander, mint and Thai basil

100g red onion, peeled and sliced

15g piece of ginger, peeled and sliced into fine julienne

15g spring onions, sliced diagonally

5g stem of lemon grass, sliced very finely

2 tomatoes, deseeded and julienned

5g red chillies, sliced diagonally

15ml Thai fish sauce (from any good Asian shop)

juice of 3 limes

6 lime wedges

I tbsp oil

Pan-fry or grill steaks for 1 minute on each side until rare, remove from pan and leave to cool. When cool, slice at an angle into 2mm strips.

Wash and drain lettuce leaves.

Pick and tear herb leaves, mix, and reserve 6 sprigs of coriander.

In a large bowl, mix together beef, red onion, ginger, spring onion, lemon grass, tomato, chillies and mixed herbs. Toss together until well mixed. Into this add the fish sauce and lime juice; mix through again.

Arrange lettuce leaves on four plates, divide beef into four and place on the lettuce; garnish with coriander sprigs and a lime wedge.

This salad does not require seasoning due to the high salinity of the fish sauce.

Photograph on page 27.

CHILLI BEEF RAMEN

4 x 150g sirloin steaks

200g fresh egg noodles

150g baby pak choi

2 litres good clear
   chicken stock

2 tbsp soy sauce

20g spring onions, finely
   sliced

20g chilli, finely sliced

For the marinade:

30ml soy sauce

10g ginger, chopped

5g garlic, sliced

10g chillies, sliced

10g coriander, chopped

10g sugar

For the chilli paste:

10g coriander

10g ginger

10g garlic

10g chilli

salt and pepper

For the chilli paste: Blend all ingredients in a kitchen blender or mortar and pestle.

Place sirloin steaks in marinade ingredients, overnight if possible.

Season and grill or pan-fry the steaks to your liking.

Cook egg noodles in boiling water for 2-3 minutes, drain and divide between four large deep bowls.

Cut pak choi lengthways, wash and discard the base stem. Place on top of noodles. Slice steak at an angle and place on top of pak choi.

Boil chicken stock and add 2 tablespoons of chilli paste and soy sauce. Taste and season. Pour stock over the beef and noodles.

Garnish with finely sliced spring onions, chilli and pickled ginger – 5g of each per person.

COD IN TAMARIND SAUCE

4 x 200g fillets of cod
flour (to coat fish)
salt and pepper
oil
1 head of chinese leaves,
    washed and chopped
    into 2.5cm cubes
10 leaves pak choi
2 litres water

1 clove of garlic, finely
    sliced
5g ginger, peeled and in
    fine julienne
15g carrot, finely diced
15g courgette, finely diced
15g aubergine, finely
    diced
15g red pepper, finely
    diced

1 small onion, finely diced
2 spring onions, sliced at
    an angle

For the sauce:

1 x 200g tamarind pulp
100g sugar
30ml vinegar
15ml Thai fish sauce

For the sauce (this can be made in advance):

Place tamarind pulp into 2 litres of warm water and leave to stand for half an hour. When soft, use both hands to knead tamarind in order to extract seeds, leaving pulp in the water. When all the seeds are relatively free from pulp, strain liquid through a coarse sieve to collect and discard seeds. Put liquid into a pot and add sugar, vinegar and Thai fish sauce, bring to the boil and simmer until the sauce is a good consistency. It should reduce by half. Taste and add more sugar if required – it should taste both bitter and sweet.

Coat fish in flour, season and fry in a little oil (they can also be poached or grilled if preferred). Keep warm.

Quickly blanch the chinese leaves and pak choi for about 1 minute in a colander and keep warm.

In a wok add a little oil and fry garlic and ginger gently. Add rest of diced vegetables and cook for 1 minute. Add about 500ml of tamarind sauce and bring to the boil. Taste for sweetness, add spring onions. Keep warm.

On four plates, put some chinese leaves and pak choy in the centre, place a fillet of cod on top, cover fish and cabbage with tamarind sauce, and garnish with spring onions.

MULLED BERRY WINE

3 leaves of gelatine

2 star anise

1 vanilla pod (split)

1 cinnamon stick

3 cloves

250ml red wine

250ml water

100g castor sugar

100g raspberries

100g blueberries

100g blackberries

100g strawberries

4 wonton

50g Mascarpone

4 sprigs mint

Soften gelatine in a little cold water for 10 minutes. Drain water and squeeze gelatine dry.

Simmer spices in wine and water for about 10 minutes. Discard spices. Dissolve sugar and taste. Add more sugar to taste, if required. Add gelatine. Leave to sit for 15 minutes. Stir well.

Sort and wash berries. Pat dry with kitchen paper. Arrange berries in four large Martini glasses. Pour cooled liquid over the fruits until just covered. Place in the fridge for 4 hours to set.

Deep-fry the wonton skin in some oil until golden. Drain on kitchen paper and sprinkle with castor sugar while warm.

To serve: Place the wonton into the jelly upright. Garnish with a spoon of Mascarpone cheese and a sprig of mint.

Photograph on page 31.

SEUMAS MacINNES

CAFÉ GANDOLFI

'If I am ever really stressed about anything, I cook. It always clears my head.'

Since the first *Glasgow on a Plate*, I've opened another Café: a franchise in Habitat in Glasgow's new shopping centre, the Buchanan Galleries. The great thing is that they asked me (not the other way around) and, for me, it's a very gentle way of expanding. I have got great staff there, and a wonderful chef, Robert Smeaton. Robert's a very inventive chef; not only is his food full of flavour, but it's also so elegantly presented.

I have always been lucky with my chefs in Albion Street too, especially with Margaret Clarence who has been with Café Gandolfi for years. She is an intuitive and natural cook. It is great to be surrounded by all this talent; there are always things you can learn from such people.

My big passion is Scottish produce, but I still find it difficult to get hold of the quality of produce I want, and new products that are coming on the market. I think if we are serious about selling Scotland as a tourist destination, we need to take pride in our culture. And isn't food so much of an important part of that culture?

I am keen to emphasise the fun of food. Don't be precious about it! People are learning and experimenting with food all the time. Take some courage; the more you do, the more you enjoy, and the better you get. If I am ever really stressed about anything, I cook. It always clears my head.

Plans for the future include writing and publishing my own style cookery book with poetry and songs – in both Gaelic and English – related to food. I have been planning a Café Gandolfi cookery book for so long, now it feels great to be finally tackling it.

GOAT'S CHEESE TART

olive oil

2 large onions, finely sliced in half-
    moons

splash of balsamic vinegar

1 egg yolk, beaten lightly

300g goat's cheese, sliced into 4

300g good-quality butter puff pastry

rocket leaves

walnut oil

lemon juice

walnut halves, to garnish

Heat enough olive oil in a frying pan to cook onion slices gently. They should not brown too much, but be sweet and transparent. This should take about 30 minutes. Then splash with balsamic vinegar and allow to cool.

Preheat the oven to 220°C (gas mark 7).

Roll out pastry to approximately 10mm thick and, using a saucer, cut out 4 discs.

Chill for 10 minutes on a baking tray.

Mix a little water with the egg yolk and brush each pastry round, leaving a border.

Place 1 dessertspoon of sautéed onions in the centre and top each with a slice of goat's cheese.

Chill for a further 10 minutes.

To cook the tart, place in preheated oven for 10 minutes or until golden in colour.

Serve on a bed of rocket leaves with a light drizzle of walnut oil and a squeeze of lemon juice.

If you like, garnish with a few walnut halves.

GRILLED SEA BASS
WITH BEETROOT RISOTTO

50g butter

1 tbsp olive oil

1 medium red onion, finely chopped

320g beetroot, cooked and chopped
(but not too finely)

350g risotto rice (arborio)

2 large beef tomatoes, skinned,
deseeded and chopped

approximately 1.2 litres good vegetable
or chicken stock

$\frac{1}{2}$ tsp salt

2 handfuls shredded fresh basil

8 fillets sea bass with the skin on (each
person should have approximately
175-200g)

deep-fried basil leaves, to garnish
(deep-fry in vegetable oil in a small
pan; takes only a few seconds)

basil oil, to drizzle (basil oil is made by
finely chopping 20g basil and 1 clove
garlic and placing in a bowl. Pour
over 150ml warmed olive oil and
leave overnight to infuse. Strain
before using.)

Melt half the butter and 1 tablespoon of oil in a large, deep frying pan and cook onion gently for 10 minutes.

Add half the beetroot and cook for 2-3 minutes.

Add rice and cook gently for 5 minutes, stirring frequently.

Then add half the tomatoes and a ladleful of hot stock.

Add salt and cook slowly, stirring frequently until the liquid is absorbed.

Continue cooking, adding a ladleful of hot stock when required, until the rice is swollen and just cooked (15-17 minutes).

Add the remaining beetroot and tomatoes, adjust seasoning, continue cooking for a further 5 minutes then take off the heat and add remaining butter and shredded basil.

Meanwhile season fish and brush with olive oil and place skin side down on a hot frying pan until skin is crisp and flesh is just cooked.

To serve, place the risotto on a warm plate and criss-cross with the sea bass. Drizzle the fish and plate with the basil oil and garnish with the deep-fried basil.

Photograph on page 35.

SLOW-SIMMERED LAMB SHANKS
WITH CHILLI JUNIPER BERRIES AND CRÈME FRAICHE

4 lamb shanks

3 tbsp olive oil

4 cloves of garlic, crushed

10 juniper berries, crushed with the
   back of a knife

2 level tsp dried chilli flakes

50g dried porcini mushrooms

300ml red wine

150ml water

700g passata

juice of 1 lemon

2 onions, roughly chopped

175g mushrooms, sliced

salt and pepper

4 tbsp crème fraiche

25g butter

Place a frying pan over a high heat and brown the lamb shanks in 2 tablespoons of olive oil, which will take 2-3 minutes each.

Now place them in a baking dish and add garlic, juniper berries, chilli flakes, dried porcini mushrooms, red wine, water, passata, lemon juice and chopped onions.

Season with salt and pepper. Cover and bake at 160°C (gas mark 3) for 2 hours.

Remove the cover and add the crème fraiche and continue cooking for 20 minutes or until lamb is very tender.

Place butter in a frying pan with 1 tablespoon olive oil and fry sliced mushrooms; do not over-colour, but allow the moisture to evaporate.

Remove lamb from dish and keep warm. Now strain the contents of dish and keep liquid warm in a pan, adding the cooked mushrooms to the sauce.

Put the lamb shanks back into the finished sauce in the pan and serve.

This dish goes well with mashed potatoes or with soft polenta and green beans.

PRUNE & BRANDY ICE CREAM

150g stoned prunes, chopped

150ml brandy

4 egg yolks

100g castor sugar

250ml double cream

250ml milk

Half vanilla pod split lengthwise or 1 tsp vanilla extract

Marinade chopped prunes in brandy overnight.

Whisk egg yolks and sugar until thick and light in colour.

Put milk and cream in a pan until hot and then gradually pour into the yolks and sugar mixture, stirring continuously. Now clean the pan and place the mixture back into the cleaned pan.

Add vanilla pod and bring mixture to just below boiling point, stirring continuously, until mixture coats the back of a wooden spoon.

Remove from the heat and place pan directly in a cold bain-marie (a deep roasting tin full of water and ice, to cool the mixture quickly), stirring occasionally. Allow to cool and then strain mixture into an ice-cream machine or a suitable container and freeze, stirring every so often to prevent ice crystals forming.

When ice cream is half-frozen, add prunes and brandy, mix well and continue to freeze overnight, until hard.

DEREK MARSHALL

GAMBA

'Fish has got to be kept really simple; you should never overpower it.'

Gamba has been open for two years now. When we first opened, we weren't sure it was going to be a success. To be honest, there are a lot of people who don't really like fish, unless it's from a chippie! So we thought we were taking a bit of a chance, but it's been great.

People are more interested in healthy eating now, and see fish as a healthy option to red meat – which, of course, it is. I think it's also down to people going on holiday to Mediterranean countries, and further afield, and trying different fish. Like sea bass and snapper, both of which we cook with here. It's as though going out to eat at a fish restaurant brings back holiday memories. I would always recommend that people buy fish from a fishmonger's; you get a better quality and selection of fish. If you go to a good fishmonger you can buy sea bass and sea bream, and they'll clean it for you and take it off the bone.

Fish is one of the simplest things to cook and it's so quick. Some people used to cook fish for ages, or boil it in milk for fifteen minutes, but they just didn't realise that you don't have to do that. Fish has got to be kept really simple; you should never overpower it. Vegetables are an ideal accompaniment, even fruit is really nice, but a sauce should always be light.

Gamba is great at what it produces, and the food is of a very high standard.

We've had the same team here for a while now, which helps us give consistent quality of food and service. I think it's very important to get the best out of your team: we try to make sure that the staff get a reasonable amount of time off each week.

As time goes on, I'd like to do something a bit different. I would love to open a Café Gamba and serve fish teas; more traditional fast food. I'm not sure about the polystyrene trays though!

PRAWN COCKTAIL
WITH STRAIGHT MALT WHISKY

300g peeled, cooked frozen prawns

3 egg yolks

3 tsp white wine vinegar

1 tsp English mustard

1/2 tsp salt

375ml vegetable oil or olive oil

2 tbsp Heinz tomato ketchup

1 tbsp malt whisky

1/2 tsp Tabasco

1 1/2 tsp Lea & Perrins

120g cos lettuce

1 lemon

Defrost prawns overnight in fridge.

Take a bowl and whisk egg yolks, vinegar, mustard and salt together. Continue to whisk and gently pour in oil to make mayonnaise. Add tomato ketchup, whisky, Tabasco and Lea & Perrins.

Finely chop cos lettuce and divide into six cold glasses; place prawns on top.

Pour sauce over prawns and serve with a wedge of lemon.

NB If you do not want to make your own mayonnaise, ensure you use a good-quality one as an alternative.

Photograph on page 43.

SMOKED SALMON OMELETTE
WITH WATERCRESS CREAM

12 eggs

$^{1}/_{2}$ tsp salt

$^{1}/_{2}$ tsp white pepper

275ml white wine

275ml fish stock

275ml double cream

1 bunch watercress, finely chopped

4 tbsp olive oil

275g smoked salmon

Whisk eggs together, adding salt and pepper, and chill.

Put white wine in a thick-bottomed pan and reduce by half. Once reduced add fish stock and reduce by half again. Add double cream, bring to the boil slowly, add watercress and simmer for 10 minutes approximately.

Remove sauce from heat and liquidise; pass through a sieve and return to a very low heat.

Heat omelette pan and when very warm add 1 tablespoon of olive oil. Swirl round and add enough omelette mix for one. Keep moving mix around with fork and when starting to cook, cover bottom of pan and add quarter of smoked salmon. Fold omelette over and place on to plate. Cover with watercress sauce and serve. Repeat for each omelette.

NB This could be used as a starter with half the recipe quantities. If so, use a small omelette pan.

WHOLE LEMON SOLE MEUNIÈRE

4 lemon sole (175-225g each)

$^1/_2$ cup plain flour

salt and ground white pepper

4 tbsp olive oil

100g unsalted butter

2 lemons

chopped fresh parsley

Trim lemon sole by removing head, fins and tail. The fishmonger will do this for you while he is removing the brown skin.

Place flour on a tray or large plate. Sprinkle fish with salt and pepper, and pat with flour, covering completely; shake off excess flour.

Heat 2 tablespoons of oil and half the butter in a large pan (big enough for 2 fish) over a medium heat. When it has melted sauté the fish on both sides till golden brown. Remove and place on a baking tray. Repeat for other 2 fish.

Add the juice of 1 lemon to the browned butter in the pan, remove from heat and add chopped parsley.

Pour butter mix over fish and bake in oven at 180°C (gas mark 4) for approximately 10 minutes.

Garnish with wedges of lemon.

POACHED PEARS
WITH MARSALA, CINNAMON AND CLOVES

4 firm pears

275ml red wine

275ml Marsala wine

225g castor sugar

1 cinnamon stick

2 cloves

ice cream/single cream, to serve

Peel the pears, leaving the stems on. Put in a pan with the wines, sugar, cinnamon stick and cloves. Bring to the boil; turn down to a simmer and cover with a lid.

Poach the pears gently for 40-45 minutes, then cool in the liquid.

When cold, remove the pears and return the poaching liquor to a fast boil, reducing by half. Allow this syrup to cool, then return the pears to it. Coat the pears with the syrup and leave to soak overnight.

Ideally serve with ice cream or pouring cream.

CALUM MATHESON

TWO FAT LADIES

'Everything we serve in Two Fat Ladies is fresh, delivered on a daily basis and cooked and eaten that night.'

I started cooking straight after I left school. I began work as a waiter in a local country club, and after six months asked to be transferred to the kitchen – that was where all the fun seemed to be! I was very lucky to get my next job at Gleneagles – what an eye-opener, working in a kitchen with over seventy chefs. Like all novice chefs, I spent my first few weeks making soup, but in time I was allowed to move from section to section, learning my trade. I then had the privilege to work for a couple of years at the Dorchester with the maestro Anton Mossiman. In all the time I worked there, I don't think I heard him raise his voice to anyone, in fact just the reverse: each morning, he went around, and shook everyone's hand; he even remembered their name.

My first job as head chef was at the Groucho Club in Soho where I had a very enjoyable and rewarding five year stay. On one occasion I organised Madonna's birthday bash, and another time, Princess Diana's lunch with Wayne Sleep.

I came to Glasgow at the end of the 1980s, and took over this restaurant – the name's derived from a bingo call: 88 Two Fat Ladies! It was very lucky find. The restaurant had been going for four years, and already had a reputation for serving good quality fresh seafood. It was ideal for a chef/patron like me, allowing me to put into practise all the knowledge, skill and (of course) love of food I had developed over the years. The interior of the restaurant is intimate, which adds to the relaxed and comfortable ambience. Like all chefs I'd like a bigger kitchen, but this one has a window on to the street – natural light is a great help.

Everything we serve in Two Fat Ladies is fresh, delivered on a daily basis and cooked and eaten that night. People can be nervous about eating seafood, but we find that once they've sampled our menu they go home with new conviction to try more fish.

PAN-FRIED SQUID
WITH GARLIC AND HERB YOGHURT

50ml organic natural yoghurt

20g chopped fresh dill/coriander or
   parsley/mint

450g cleaned fresh squid, cut in 0.5cm
   rings

75g plain flour

25ml olive oil

$^1/_2$ clove of garlic, chopped

salt and pepper to taste

1 lemon, cut into quarters and
   deseeded

Pre-prepare the herb yoghurt by mixing the yoghurt and herbs together, allowing time for the herbs to flavour the mixture (about 8 hours).

This can be done the day before, or in the morning.

Coat squid rings in flour, shaking off any excess. Add to a pan with medium-hot oil then turn to high. It is vital not to pile all the squid into the frying pan; usually 2-3 batches will be sufficient. Fry for 2-3 minutes each side, adding chopped garlic 1 minute from the end; at this point you might need to add more oil if necessary. Season and serve with a wedge of lemon.

Photograph on page 51.

BAKED FILLET OF SEA BASS
WITH SESAME SEEDS AND TERIYAKI SAUCE

For the pickled carrot/cucumber

25g carrot

25g cucumber

1 tbsp water

2 tbsp rice vinegar

Dash of soy sauce

30g plain flour

40g sesame seeds

25ml sunflower oil

4 x 200g sea bass fillet

125ml teriyaki sauce

1 lemon

For the pickled carrot/cucumber: cut carrot and cucumber into 3cm chunks, and then into thin slices (remove all seeds from cucumber).

Mix water, vinegar and soy sauce together and marinade carrot and cucumber slices for a few hours or longer.

Mix together plain flour and sesame seeds.

Dip clean fillets into sesame seed and flour mixture.

Heat the oil in a heavy-bottomed pan.

Lightly fry sea bass for about 1 minute on each side then add the teriyaki sauce.

Bake in the oven at 175ºC (gas mark 3-4) for 4-5 minutes.

Serve with lemon wedges and pickled vegetables.

SCOTTISH LOBSTER & MELON SALAD

WITH TOMATO AND CORIANDER SALSA

For the grain mustard and honey dressing:

1 tbsp French grain mustard

1 tsp honey

2 tsp white wine vinegar

1 tsp balsamic vinegar

250ml olive oil

For the plum tomato salsa:

225g plum tomatoes, diced

50g coriander, chopped

1/2 red chilli, chopped

1/2 green chilli, chopped

1 small/medium red onion, chopped

dash of balsamic vinegar

dash of white wine vinegar

juice of $1/2$ lemon

500g cooked lobster

1 medium galia melon, cut, deseeded, peeled and sliced

2 tsp extra virgin olive oil

200g mixed leaves: rocket, lollo rosso and oak, well washed and drained

1 lemon

Cut lobster tails in half, taking out the long thin intestine.

Slice tails and neatly place on top of the melon. Along with the tails use 1 claw and 2 knuckles per portion. Drizzle the extra virgin oil over the top.

Mix the salad leaves with the dressing (mix all ingredients well in a lidded jar) and share out.

Add a couple of spoonfuls of plum tomato salsa and a lemon wedge.

This dish goes well with lovely new potatoes with fresh mint.

PAVLOVA WITH DRAMBUIE
FLAMBÉD BERRIES AND CREAM

For the pavlova:

2 fresh egg whites

Pinch of salt

100g castor sugar

1 level tsp corn flour

$^1/_2$ tsp white wine vinegar

3-4 drops of vanilla essence

25g butter

40g soft brown sugar

350g (total) mixed berries (strawberries, raspberries
    and blackcurrants)

40ml Drambuie

100ml double cream, whipped

Pavlova is a soft meringue with a crisp outer coating. Cook for $1^1/_2$ hours in a preheated oven at 150°C (gas mark $2^1/_4$), turning twice, till light brown in colour.

Whisk egg whites and salt on high speed till stiff (about 2-3 minutes).

Add the castor sugar one spoon at a time, slowly and evenly around the bowl. The meringue should have doubled in volume.

Then on a slow speed add corn flour, vinegar and vanilla essence.

Spoon individual mounds of meringue mix on to greaseproof paper and pop in the preheated oven as described above.

Leave to cool for 5 minutes before lifting the meringues from the tray.

Melt butter and brown sugar on medium heat, then add mixed berries. Turn heat up to high and sauté for 1 minute. Reduce heat and add the Drambuie, turn heat up high again and flambé for another minute. Stand well back when adding the liqueur. The berries should still have some bite and shape to them. Serve with whipped cream and pavlova on the top.

RICHARD MILLER

MALMAISON

'We aim to provide real food of a consistently high quality at an affordable price.'

When I was at school, I wanted to be a physical

education teacher, but in sixth year, I studied food and nutrition, and much to my surprise, loved it. I decided then that I wanted to be a chef. I was playing a lot of football and had made it to quite a serious level, so all my friends were a bit surprised – there were more than a few raised eyebrows – cooking wasn't quite what they expected.

I'm from the far north of Scotland, from Brora in Sutherland, and after school I went to college in Inverness for two years. But to be honest I couldn't wait to stop studying and start real work. So I left college early and went to work in a seafood restaurant in Ullapool. All the fresh produce was right on our doorstep – we had deliveries of fish straight from the trawlers every night.

I've been at Malmaison, Glasgow, for three years now and was recently promoted to Head Chef. After working in smaller kitchens and small restaurants, it can be quite daunting to work in a bigger one, and in such a fast paced Brasserie environment. But I love it. When you're the boss, you're responsible for bringing all sorts of personalities together as a team, constantly and consistently giving them the sort of support and leadership that they need to perform at their highest level every minute of the day.

The food at Malmaison has its origins deeply rooted in traditional French Brasseries, but then we interpret the dishes and the cooking techniques in a much more contemporary style. Always using the freshest of seasonal produce, changing the menus throughout the year to mirror that ethos. We aim to provide real food of a consistently high quality at an affordable price.

My ambition is to establish myself as head chef at Malmaison Glasgow, under the guidance of our group Executive Chef, Roy Brett. For the moment, that's a big enough challenge, and cooking great food, with a great team, for an awful lot of happy people, is a big enough reward.

MALMAISON PRAWN COCKTAIL

300g king prawns

50g butter

2 cloves of garlic

2 eggs

300g pak choi

$^1/_2$ lemon

40g chives

Marie Rose Sauce

150g mayonnaise

50g tomato ketchup

4 dashes of Tabasco

2 tbsp Worcester sauce

1 tsp lemon juice

Add the butter and garlic to water then add the prawns, heating them until they are lightly poached.

Hard boil eggs, peel and grate finely.

To prepare marie rose sauce, combine all ingredients in a bowl until thoroughly mixed.

Prepare pak choi by finely shredding green leaves and julienne the white stalks.

Pour a little marie rose sauce into the bottom of 4 martini glasses.

In a bowl, season pak choi with the juice of $^1/_2$ lemon and finely chopped chives and then place into the glasses.

In a separate bowl mix together prawns with grated egg and the rest of marie rose sauce. Then place on top of pak choi to serve.

SALAD NIÇOISE

250g new potatoes

salt and pepper

1g saffron strands

1 medium red onion

100g green beans

75ml olive oil

75g fresh basil

12 quails eggs

100g cherry tomatoes

200g tuna

75g chervil

Top and tail potatoes, turning them into barrel shapes then cook softly in seasoned water flavoured with saffron, for 12-15 minutes depending on size.

Peel the red onion then slice thinly into rings.

Top and tail green beans then blanch in seasoned boiling water. Leave for a minute and then strain. Place immediately into iced water until chilled. Drain well then split lengthways in half.

Add 50ml olive oil to basil, purée with hand blitzer and season to taste.

Place eggs in a small saucepan with cold water and bring to boil; once boiling, take from heat, refresh under cold water and when cold peel eggs gently.

In a mixing bowl put red onion rings, cherry tomatoes, green beans, quails eggs and potatoes and toss carefully in the basil oil.

Place a 100mm-pastry cutter in the centre of the plate, then place salad in the ring. Remove ring.

Dress tuna with remainder of oil and place into a hot griddle. Pan-fry on both sides, keeping tuna pink in the middle. Place tuna, once cooked, on salad and garnish with chervil.

PAN-FRIED SEA BREAM
WITH CHAR-GRILLED SWEET POTATOES

500g sweet potatoes

100ml olive oil

salt and pepper

250g plum tomatoes

1 medium red onion

75g parsley

2 medium lemons

1 kg sea bream fillets x 4

Thinly slice potatoes into rounds, dress with half the oil, season and then fry in the griddle pan. Mark them on one side and then to complete cooking, finish them in the oven for a further 5 minutes at 200°C.

Deseed and chop tomatoes into small dice then peel onion and chop to same size as tomato.

Roughly chop parsley, mix with tomatoes and red onion then squeeze juice of one lemon into the mix. Add 50ml olive oil and season, mix well and keep salsa in fridge.

Brush sea bream fillets with oil and season with salt and pepper. Place skin-side down in a hot frying pan and cook for about 2 minutes. Then turn and cook for a further 2 minutes. Once cooked keep hot.

To serve place 2 teaspoons of salsa mix in the centre of the plate, add hot potato slices on to salsa, then place fish on top.

Garnish with a lemon wedge and sprig of chervil.

CHOCOLATE TART
WITH WHITE CHOCOLATE ICE CREAM
AND A CHOCOLATE TUILLE

The Tart	White Chocolate Ice Cream	Chocolate Tuille mix
500g butter	250ml milk	25g plain flour
450g icing sugar	250ml double cream	10g dark cocoa powder
1 kilo plain flour	125g castor sugar	25g egg white (approx 2
7 eggs	250g white chocolate	eggs)
800g chocolate (min. 64%	1 vanilla pod	30g butter
cocoa solids)	5 egg yolks	40g icing sugar
900g Mascarpone	375ml semi-whipped	
100g castor sugar	double cream	

For the Tart: Rub together butter, icing sugar and flour. Work in 3 eggs and knead into pastry. Rest for at least 30 minutes. Roll pastry into tart base and cook blind. Remove beans and continue cooking until base is dry and firm. Leave to cool. Melt chocolate and Mascarpone in separate bain-maries. Add castor sugar to Mascarpone then beat in 4 eggs. Mix well then pour in melted chocolate. Stir until smooth. Pour into cooled tart base and put in fridge to set. This will take 3-4 hours. Cut using a hot knife.

    For the Chocolate Tuille mix: Place all ingredients in a food processor and mix well into a paste. Get a 5cm circular flat template. Place a sheet of silicon paper on a baking tray. Take template and place onto tray, then spread the mix thinly and evenly into the template. Cook in the oven at 220°C (gas mark 7) for about 2-3 minutes, take out and leave to cool. Be careful, as they are very brittle and easily broken. To serve, place a wedge of tart on the plate, put a tuille beside it and a scoop of ice cream on top of the tuille.

    For the White Chocolate Ice Cream: Bring milk and cream to the boil. In a bowl whisk yolks, sugar and the seed of $1/2$ vanilla pod together. Take a ladle of cream and milk mixture and whisk into egg yolk mix to thin down. Bring a pan of water to a simmering heat. Fill a pyrex bowl with the cream mix, place over hot water and bring to boil. Then add in egg yolk mix. Stir this constantly until mix is thick enough to coat the back of a wooden spoon. When it is ready take off the heat. Whisk in white chocolate to the mix, allow to cool and then gently fold through the semi-whipped cream. Churn in an ice cream maker for 20-25 minutes. Put into an airtight container and place in freezer.

Photograph on page 59.

MARTIN MOCHAN

LA FIORENTINA

'I always enjoy watching people indulge themselves, knowing it was my hands that created each dish.'

When I left school in 1986, I was totally undecided

about what I would like to do. I went to see my careers officer, who suggested the catering industry. Despite the fact that beans on toast was my speciality, I decided there was no harm in trying.

I was given a placement as a YTS and my first job was in a small Country Club. I discovered I had a natural talent for cooking, and for making it look good. One of my favourite jobs at the club was preparing the buffets, making sure the food looked beautiful.

After nine months I felt I needed a new challenge, and it was then I was given a new placement at an Italian restaurant, the famous Piccolo Mondo in Renfrew. I still remember the excitement I felt when I first started there; I owe a lot to Antonio and Giuliana Pierotti. I learned the fine art of Italian cooking, enjoying making all the dishes and sauces; I always enjoy watching people indulge themselves, knowing it was my hands that created each dish.

In 1992 the Pierotti family put their trust in me and gave me the chance to prove myself as head chef in their new restaurant, La Riviera. After years of someone else being in charge, I was the one giving instructions, and here was my chance to put everything I had learned into practice. Very scary indeed, but it was a great success.

When La Riviera was sold, in 1995, I joined the Pierotti family at La Fiorentina as head chef. I was then promoted to executive chef. I now feel part of an Italian family and the typical Italian nature has rubbed off on me: I'm such a perfectionist! Who would have thought that a young Scottish lad brought up on mince and potatoes would be able to gain the knowledge and skill I have over the years? Working with wonderful raw ingredients, magical colours and fabulous flavours to tantalise the taste buds, which when carefully added together make very healthy dishes for everyone to enjoy (including me, of course!).

MEDITERRANEAN ANTIPASTO

3 peppers: 1 green, 1 red, 1 yellow

400g button mushrooms, whole

200g wild mushrooms

1 large courgette

1 large aubergine

1 large onion

1 tsp salt

$1/2$ tsp black pepper

2 cloves of garlic, sliced thin

$1/2$ fresh chilli

12 basil leaves, roughly chopped

4 tbsp extra virgin olive oil

300g salad leaves including endives and
    rocket

2 x 125g packets baby Mozzarella

Balsamic vinegar

Preheat chargrill to 200°C (gas mark 6).

Place whole peppers on grill, add a touch of oil, cook evenly until pepper skins are black.

Remove peppers and place in a sealed plastic tub. Leave for $1/2$ hour until cool, then skin will peel off easily.

Deseed and slice lengthways as desired.

Grill both kinds of mushrooms as above, turning until cooked.

Slice courgette, aubergine and onion thinly lengthways and grill.

When all veg are cooled, place on shallow dish and season with salt and pepper, garlic, chilli, basil and oil.

Chop salad leaves (preferably endives). Place on middle of serving plate, assemble antipasto on leaves. Slice Mozzarella, place on top, garnish with rocket leaves and dress with a little balsamic vinegar.

Photograph on page 67.

ESCALOPE OF VEAL RIFATTA

(MEANS COOKED TWICE)

250ml extra virgin olive oil

2 eggs

75ml full-cream milk

500g veal topside

125g white breadcrumbs

For the sauce:

5 tbsp extra virgin olive oil

2 cloves of garlic, crushed

25g fresh parsley, chopped

1kg tinned, peeled plum tomatoes

2 pinches of salt, 2 pinches of pepper

2 chicken stock cubes

75g Flora margarine

250ml water

Put oil in a shallow frying pan on a medium heat. Crack eggs in a bowl, add milk and mix well. Place veal in egg mix and then gently coat with breadcrumbs. When oil is hot, turn heat down, and fry veal until golden brown on both sides (about 1 minute each side).

For the sauce: Place frying pan on medium heat. Add oil, garlic, parsley and fry gently to release the flavours. Add tomatoes, salt and pepper, stock cubes, margarine and water. Leave to simmer for 10–15 minutes. Taste, and add more seasoning if required.

To serve, pour sauce over veal and accompany with creamed potatoes and mangetout.

FILETTINI DI POLLO ALLA DUCHESSA
DUCHESS-STYLE FILLETS OF BREAST OF CHICKEN

4 x 175g chicken breasts

60g plain flour

150ml extra virgin olive oil

salt

white pepper

150ml glass white wine

500ml cold water

2 chicken stock cubes

1 whole lemon

60g capers

1kg potatoes, cleaned

75ml milk

100g Flora margarine

16 asparagus spears

200g tagliolini pasta

flat-leaf parsley, to garnish

Cut each chicken breast into 4 pieces and bash each piece gently with a meat tenderiser till flat, then dip into 10g flour, lightly coating each side. Heat 30ml extra virgin olive oil in a large frying pan on medium heat till warm, then add chicken pieces. Sprinkle with salt and pepper. Fry chicken for about 1 minute on each side. Lower heat, then sprinkle 50g plain flour evenly over the chicken. Mix until you have a light roux, turning chicken pieces at the same time. Add white wine, then water and sprinkle chicken cubes over, mixing well. Add $1/4$ of lemon juice and the capers to sauce. Simmer for a few minutes until sauce thickens, then remove from heat. Add seasoning to taste.

Put the potatoes in a good-sized pot. Cover with water, add a pinch of salt. Bring to boil, then turn down heat and simmer until cooked. Strain. Return potatoes to pan and mash, adding milk and Flora margarine. Season to taste.

Using a medium-sized pot fill $2/3$ with water. Bring to boil. Squeeze $1/4$ of lemon juice into water, add 1 teaspoon of salt, then add asparagus. Boil for about 5 minutes until tender, then strain.

Fill a medium-sized pot with water, add 1 teaspoon of salt and 75ml extra virgin olive oil. Bring to boil, then add the pasta mixing it occasionally for 1 minute, then take off and strain. Just in case, always check the packet for cooking instructions as these may differ.

To serve, pipe mashed potatoes on to the four corners of the plate. Put tagliolini into the centre of the plate with asparagus between each of the mashed potatoes. Place the chicken round the tagliolini then pour the sauce lightly over the chicken and pasta. Garnish with flat-leaf parsley.

MARTIN MOCHAN

TIRAMISU

2 eggs, separated

250g Mascarpone cheese, at room temperature

a few drops of vanilla essence

2 tbsp castor sugar

175ml very strong black coffee

2 tbsp Marsala

1 tbsp brandy

2 tbsp Sambuca

150g Savoiardi sponge fingers

1 tbsp cocoa powder

chocolate flake or Ferrero Rocher chocolates, to decorate

The name of this popular dessert translates as 'pick me up', which is said to derive from the fact that it is so good that it literally makes you swoon when you eat it. There are many many versions, and the recipe can be adapted to suit your own taste – you can vary the amount of Mascarpone, eggs, sponge fingers, coffee and liqueur.

Put egg whites in a grease-free bowl and whisk with an electric mixer until stiff in peaks.

Mix Mascarpone, vanilla essence and egg yolks in a separate large bowl and whisk with the electric mixer until evenly combined.

Fold in egg whites, then put a few spoonfuls of the mixture in the bottom of a large serving bowl and spread it out evenly.

Mix coffee and liqueur together in a shallow dish. Dip a sponge finger in the mixture, turn it quickly so that it becomes saturated but does not disintegrate, and place it on top of Mascarpone mixture in the bowl. Add five more dipped sponge fingers, placing them side by side.

Spoon in about one-third of the remaining mixture and spread it out.

Make more layers in the same way, ending with Mascarpone.

Level the surface, then sift cocoa powder all over. For best results cover and chill overnight (although 1 hour will do).

Before serving, sprinkle with cocoa and grated chocolate flake, or whole Ferrero Rocher.

Use your imagination in your choice of liqueur and decoration!

MONIR MOHAMMED

MOTHER INDIA

'I've often said to people that if you are going to eat Indian food, eat before 10 o'clock!'

I started working when I was fourteen. My brother opened a restaurant in Bathgate, and I used to go down at the weekends to help in the kitchen. I started off doing the general things, washing dishes, peeling onions and chopping salads. I found the noise and the atmosphere in the kitchen so exciting, even though I was told not to get too involved and to concentrate on my studies. At that time, working in a restaurant was not seen as much of a career.

I started working in the Ashoka in 1982, which had only just opened. I worked there for about seven years, and became a manager of one of their restaurants. The perception of Indian cooking is changing, although there's still a long way to go. I can remember when there used to be a rush to Indian restaurants at about eleven thirty, when the pubs closed. It's less common now; people are less inclined to eat at that time of night. I've often said to people that if you are going to eat Indian food, eat before 10 o'clock!

There are still people who are used to choosing dishes because they look nice and rich, but that could just be the food colouring. We don't use any colouring here, and cook individual, traditional dishes.

I've started doing the occasional cookery classes at Mother India. People come along and cook their own lunch. We decide a menu: starters, a main course and dessert. People then volunteer to make certain dishes: the pakoras, rice, chappaties. I keep an eye on everyone. The most important part of Indian cooking is the timing of the ingredients going into the dish. Once the cooking is all over, we all sit down and have lunch, and that's the most interesting time for me – when I get to hear what people have to say about food, and Mother India.

SPICED HADDOCK

3 tbsp vegetable oil

2 tbsp natural yoghurt

3 tbsp fresh lemon juice

$1/4$ tbsp salt

$1/2$ tbsp red chilli

$1/2$ tsp black pepper

50g fresh coriander

$1/4$ tbsp cumin

450g prime haddock

In a large bowl mix together oil, yoghurt and lemon juice then add salt, red chilli, black pepper and coriander. Heat cumin in a frying pan for 5 minutes, let it cool down, and add to the marinade, giving all the ingredients a good mix. Make sure the haddock is nice and dry and add to the mixture and let it marinade for 2-3 hours, then bake in the oven for 20 minutes at 220ºC (gas mark 7).

Photograph on page 75.

CUMIN CHICKEN WITH LADYFINGERS
WITH CUCUMBER AND RADISH RAITA

220ml vegetable oil

3 medium-size onions

8 cloves of garlic

60g fresh ginger

6 green chillies

1 tbsp cumin seeds

2 sticks of cinnamon

6 black peppercorns

4 tomatoes, finely chopped

1 tbsp salt

$^3/_4$ tbsp red chilli

$^1/_2$ tbsp tumeric

4 chicken breasts (175-225g) on the
   bone (score flesh)

50g fresh coriander

225g ladyfingers

For the raita:

$^1/_2$ cucumber

60g radish

150ml yoghurt

$^1/_2$ tsp salt

$^1/_2$ tsp mint

$^1/_4$ tsp black pepper

$^1/_2$ tsp roasted cumin

Heat vegetable oil in medium-sized pot then add onion. Grind garlic, ginger and green chilli together in a small food blender, and add to onions after 10 minutes. After a further 10 minutes add the whole spices: cumin, cinnamon, and black peppercorns. After 15 minutes add tomatoes. Once onions and tomatoes are practically dissolved, add salt, red chilli and tumeric. After 10 minutes add chicken breasts and cook on medium heat for about 35-40 minutes before adding the coriander and landyfingers. Simmer for 10 minutes and serve with the raita.

For the raita: chop cucumber and radish, add to yoghurt, then add salt, mint and black pepper. Take the cumin and put it into small frying pan, heat for 2 minutes and put on top of the raita.

PATINA GOSHT
WITH GARLIC POTATOES

150ml vegetable oil

3 onions, finely chopped

10 cloves of garlic

75-110g ginger

6 green chillies

1 tbsp cumin seeds

2 cinnamon sticks

2 black cardamom pods

2 cloves

6 whole black peppercorns

1kg lamb, diced into 3cm squares

4 tomatoes, chopped

3/4 tbsp salt

1/2 tbsp red chilli

1/4 tbsp tumeric

50g fresh coriander

50g fresh mint

Garlic Potatoes

110ml vegetable oil

1 medium-sized onion

1/2 tbsp cumin seeds

1 cinnamon stick

4 whole peppercorns

2 cloves

3 bay leaves

4 cloves of garlic

2 tomatoes, finely chopped

1/2 tbsp salt

1/2 kg baby potatoes

Heat vegetable oil in a medium-sized pot then add onion. Grind garlic and ginger together in a small food blender and then add green chillies. Process again. Add to the onions after 10 minutes. After a further 10 minutes add the whole spices: cumin, cinnamon, cardamoms, cloves and peppercorns. After 15 minutes add lamb and tomatoes and cook for about 50 minutes, then add salt, red chilli and tumeric. After 10 minutes add coriander and mint and let it simmer a further 10 minutes.

For the Garlic Potatoes: heat oil in a pot and add onion. After 10 minutes add cumin, cinnamon, peppercorn, cloves and bay leaves. After 15 minutes add crushed garlic and cook for 15 minutes. Make sure onion, garlic and whole spices are well caramelised, then add tomatoes and salt. Cook for 10 minutes.

Boil baby potatoes 3/4 through (15-20 minutes), drain, and put in a baking tray, then smother with sauce and place in a preheated oven (220°C/gas mark 7) for 20 minutes.

KHEER
(Serves 4-6)

350g Basmati Rice
1¹/₂ litres of milk
350g sugar
4 green cardamoms
12 whole almonds
12 sultanas
Amaretto cherries (optional)

Soak the rice overnight in water.

Next day wash through and put in a heavy based pot. Cover the rice with 9cm of water and let it simmer until the water practically disappears. Then add the milk, sugar and cardamoms and cook on medium heat for 1 hour, stirring every 15 minutes. Add the almonds and sultanas at the end (we recommended serving with Amaretto cherries or fresh fruit).

DONALD ANGUS MUNRO

LOOP

'We want the restaurant to be an informal and friendly environment.'

I started out when I got a summer job working in a kitchen and got a real buzz from it; the theatre of it all, the chefs in their whites, the noise. I didn't go back to school. I went straight from school into the kitchen, but managed to start at Glasgow College of Food Technology where I gained my qualifications.

My first job was at the RAC Club where the hours were long, but a good grounding and classical training. I then moved around various five star establishments at home and abroad, gaining a wealth of experience, finally ending up as Executive Head Chef at Peter de Savary's Carnegie Club at Skibo Castle. I was sent to various destinations, including New York and Los Angeles, just to cook simple Scottish dishes for the rich and famous, who treated me as their own chef. A lot of the old recipes are becoming really fashionable again. I'm always digging out recipes my Mum and Nan used to use. In fact, the recipe for the chocolate pudding was Nana's, I just added the Macallan!

During a visit to London in 1999, I literally bumped into an old friend, Craig Johnson. Craig talked about his plans to open a restaurant in Glasgow, my hometown. As Craig's background is not in the catering industry I found his approach to ideas about eating out refreshing. The idea behind Loop was to combine my experience with his philosophy of keeping it simple. The outcome – Loop Restaurant – opened in July 1999 and a second Loop opened in August 2000.

Craig and I work well together. He constantly challenges the old-fashioned attitudes within the catering industry and that has played a significant part in Loop's success. We don't want to be fussy; we want the restaurant to be an informal and friendly environment. If you happen to put a glass on the wrong side of the table or use the wrong knife to eat your starter, then so what?, we don't mind if you don't!

Our staff are the faces of Loop, they represent us. Training and teaching are very important. If we do that properly, then our staff care about what they put on the plate, how things are presented, how the food tastes. Every new member of staff gets to taste dishes from the menu, otherwise how can they recommend anything?

Craig wants to go and live and work in the sun; maybe we'll take Loop to Australia!

CRAB & SWEETCORN SPRING ROLL

300g white crabmeat

salt and pepper

3 tbsp mustard mayonnaise (good-
quality mayonnaise mixed with
mustard of your choice)

100g cooked sweetcorn

1 tbsp basil, chopped

1 tbsp coriander, chopped

12 sheets of filo pastry (23cm square)

egg wash: 2 egg yolks beaten with 1
tsp water

sunflower oil for deep frying

oyster sauce (bought)

seasonal salad leaves, to serve

Finely flake crabmeat, season and mix with mustard mayonnaise, sweetcorn, basil and coriander.

Place a sheet of filo at an angle on the board so that one corner points towards you. Brush with egg wash, spoon in a little of the mix on the top corner, fold over and roll it towards you, folding in the sides and continue to roll up. Place on a non-stick tray. Repeat with other filo sheets.

Heat oil to 150°C and deep-fry the roll for about 3-4 minutes or until golden brown.

Drain on kitchen paper to remove excess fat.

Serve with seasonal salad leaves and oyster sauce.

Photograph on page 83.

SMOKED MACKEREL RISOTTO

1 litre chicken stock

salt and pepper

140g butter

3 tbsp olive oil

2 garlic cloves peeled and chopped

1 medium red onion, finely chopped

280g risotto rice (arborio)

50ml dry white vermouth

3 fillets of smoked mackerel (small
    pieces)

100ml double cream

224g freshly grated Parmesan

Heat chicken stock and check seasoning.

Melt half butter with half olive oil in a heavy-bottomed saucepan, fry off garlic and onion, and cook until soft. Add rice away from the heat and stir until rice becomes totally coated – takes approximately 1 minute.

Return to heat, add 2 ladles of stock and vermouth and simmer, stirring until rice has absorbed the liquid. Add more stock and stir until all the stock has been absorbed (15-20 minutes).

Add mackerel, stir and then add remaining butter, olive oil, cream and Parmesan; check seasoning and serve.

THAI CHICKEN
WITH LEMON AND MINT COUSCOUS

570ml carton natural yoghurt

1 tbsp Thai curry paste

1 bunch of coriander, chopped

1 small piece (75g) of fresh ginger,
   finely chopped

4 breasts of chicken

2 cloves of garlic, crushed

2 red chillies

1 onion

1 tin of peeled tomatoes

1 (250g) pkt of couscous

570ml of hot chicken stock

1 small bunch of fresh mint

1 lemon

salt and pepper

olive oil

Mix yoghurt, curry paste, coriander and ginger together. Coat chicken breasts with mixture and leave to rest for 24 hours.

Fry garlic, chilli and onion then add tomatoes. Cook for 2 minutes then blitz in a blender. Leave to rest.

Heat griddle pan and place chicken presentation side (flat side) down for 4 minutes. Turn and cook other side for 5 minutes or until firm to touch.

Place couscous in a bowl and pour over hot stock, stirring until it has all been absorbed – add more if necessary (it should have the appearance of bread crumbs), this takes 3-4 minutes. Chop in the mint, squeeze in the lemon juice, season to taste and add a splash of olive oil.

Serve the couscous on a hot plate. Cut the chicken breasts in two and place on top of couscous. Serve with peppers, courgettes and aubergine pan-fried with a little garlic. Add chilli sauce.

MACALLAN'S CHOCOLATE PUDDING

110g castor sugar

110g margarine

60g cocoa powder or drinking
   chocolate

170g flour

2 eggs

25ml Macallan whisky

2 tbsp skimmed milk

50g soft berries of choice

For the sauce:

140g dark chocolate (70% cocoa solids)

150ml double cream

25ml Macallan whisky

1 tbsp golden syrup

Blend sugar and margarine until light and fluffy.

Sieve cocoa powder or chocolate into flour.

Whisk eggs together then add to sugar mix, adding a little flour mix to thicken.

Add whisky and more flour mix until both flour and whisky have been used. Add skimmed milk, to soften.

Grease 4 individual pudding moulds with margarine and dust with castor sugar.

Place a spoonful of the mix into each mould, cover with tin foil and secure tightly.

Place in a pot of warm water which reaches halfway up the moulds.

Bring to the boil then simmer for 40 minutes.

For the sauce: melt chocolate in a boil over boiling water, add cream, whisky and syrup to form the sauce.

Remove puddings and place on plates then pour over the chocolate sauce, adding a few soft berries.

Serve.

FERRIER RICHARDSON

EURASIA

STEVEN CAPUTA & FERRIER RICHARDSON

'Glaswegians enjoy Chinese and Indian food, so we're not trying to convince people to eat something they don't want to.'

We've been really pleased and surprised at the way things have gone for Eurasia, in the relatively short space of time since we first discovered this office block in St Vincent Street in January 1999. The fact that we managed to open in October that year was something of a miracle, bearing in mind we had to go through planning permission and all that entails. There were, certainly, a few scary moments, but it was phenomenal to turn the whole project around in a nine-week building programme.

The way the staff have settled in highlights what my management team have achieved, and the thought that went into the design has ensured great facilities for the whole team.

We've worked very hard over the first year, and have been really fortunate that we've had great press reviews – my mother couldn't have written better ones! That really helps when people are flagging; it's bound to happen, with all the hard work and effort, and a good review can really gee up the staff, and encourage them to carry on the good work. We were delighted to win 'The New Restaurant of the Year' award – that really helped to keep us all going too.

The food is a style that's fashionable, but we haven't just jumped on the bandwagon. It's a style that's influenced me for a long time. Glaswegians enjoy Chinese and Indian food, so we're not trying to convince people to eat something they don't want to. We've got some of the best produce in the world in Scotland – cold-water fish, game, lamb and beef – and when the quality is top class as well, you have a nice marriage. Hence the name Eurasia, European-Asian, a fusion.

I would like to see Eurasia consolidate. I think we won't have to run so fast as we have over the first year. I always say to my staff that it's easier to get there, but harder to stay there. That's the key thing now, to maintain the quality. We can't become complacent.

HOT & SOUR MUSHROOM SOUP

570ml vegetable stock

5cm piece of lemon grass, crushed

4 lime leaves

1 tsp fresh ginger, finely sliced

4 tbsp lime juice

3 tbsp light soya sauce

seasoning

1 tbsp red chillies, finely sliced

75g enoki mushrooms

75g shitake mushrooms

4 tbsp coriander leaves

Bring stock to boil in pan.

Add all ingredients except mushrooms and coriander, and simmer for 10 minutes to infuse.

Remove lime leaves and lemon grass.

Steam mushrooms in four moulds and place one in centre of each soup bowl.

Remove moulds and pour soup around. Garnish with coriander.

FIVE-WAY SALMON SUSHI

Sushi
225g sushi rice
400ml water
2 tbsp white wine vinegar
1/2 tsp salt
1/2 tbsp sugar

Tempura
1 egg (medium)
100ml ice-cold water
salt and pepper
3 tbsp plain flour
1 tbsp cornflour

For Sushi: Soak rice thoroughly for 1 hour, changing water frequently. Drain, then cook in water in pot or preferably in rice cooker until grains are plump and water absorbed. Mix together vinegar, salt and sugar, fold through rice and allow to cool covered with a damp cloth.

For the tempura batter: Whisk egg, water and seasonings. Sieve flour and corn flour together.

Add flour and cornflour mixture, one quarter at a time to egg and water mixture (there should be lumps remaining). Add more iced water to dilute if required – this should make a thin batter (single cream consistency). Fry at 200°C until golden.

Prepare smoked salmon Sushi by laying a roll of Nori seaweed with rice, place a strip of cucumber and smoked salmon lengthways, roll up tightly using sushi mat or cling film. Slice.

Prepare Ketta Sushi by laying a roll of Nori seaweed with a tube of rice. Roll with sushi mat and top with Ketta.

Prepare raw salmon with a ball of sushi rice and top with slice of raw salmon.

Prepare curried salmon with a cylinder of sushi rice and top with a thin gravadlax.

Prepare Tempura salmon with a ball of sushi rice and top with deep fried piece of tempura salmon.

SEARED WEST COAST SALMON
WITH STEAMED VEGETABLES AND ORIENTAL BOUILLON

4 x 175g salmon fillets (skin on)

3 tbsp vegetable oil

8 pieces bok choi

4 large potatoes (e.g. Maris Piper), cut
into 20 1.5cm cubes

1 pinch of saffron strands

20 pieces of spring onion (white part)

For the bouillon:

425ml clear fish stock

1 tbsp finely diced chilli

1 tbsp finely diced ginger

2 tbsp shredded coriander

Sear salmon in hot frying pan with vegetable oil.

Transfer to dish and cook in oven for 17 minutes at 200ºC (gas mark 6).

Steam bok choi until tender, about 5 minutes.

Poach potato cubes in saffron and salted water until tender, but still retains shape (about 20 minutes).

Steam spring onions until tender.

For the bouillon: bring fish stock to boil and simmer with chilli and ginger for 10 minutes to infuse, then add coriander.

Place 2 pieces of bok choi in centre of each bowl, place potatoes around and top with spring onion.

Ladle bouillon over bok choi and top with salmon (skin side up). Serve immediately.

TRIO OF PINEAPPLE DESSERTS (Serves 8)

Pineapple ice cream

1 small pineapple

110g castor sugar

500ml milk

6 egg yolks

1 vanilla pod (split)

100ml double cream

Pineapple brûlée

1 small pineapple

110g castor sugar

570ml double cream

8 egg yolks

Pineapple spring rolls

1 pineapple

$1/2$ stem candied angelica
  (optional)

8 sheets spring roll pastry

2 egg whites

castor sugar for dredging

oil for deep frying

Pineapple ice cream: Peel, core and cut pineapple into small dice, add to saucepan with half the sugar and cook over a medium heat until softened. Add the milk. Whisk egg yolks with remaining sugar and vanilla pod. Bring milk mixture to a boil and whisk on to yolk mixture. Return to saucepan and reheat gently, stirring constantly until custard thickens enough to coat the back of a wooden spoon. Add cream and leave to cool. When cooled churn the custard in an ice-cream machine.

Pineapple brûlée: Peel, core and cut pineapple into small dice. Add to a saucepan with half the sugar and cook for 5 minutes on a low heat. When pineapple has softened, add the double cream. Meanwhile whisk yolks with remaining sugar. Bring cream mixture to a boil and quickly whisk into yolks. Strain mixture through a fine sieve and divide equally between ramekin dishes. Place ramekins in a water bath, cover with tin foil and bake in oven at 180°C (gas mark 4) for approximately 30-45 mnutes until set. Cool at room temperature and refrigerate for a few hours. When chilled and set, sprinkle the surface of the custards with a little more castor sugar and caramelise with a blow torch or under a hot grill.

Pineapple spring rolls: Peel, core and cut pineapple flesh into thin strips and cut the angelica into a fine julienne. Mix together and place in a clean cloth and gently squeeze to remove excess liquid juice. Lay sheets of spring roll pastry on a table and brush with egg whites, sprinkle with castor sugar and place a little of the pineapple mixture about 3cm from bottom edge on sheet of pastry. Fold the two sides of pastry lengthways over the pineapple and roll gently but tightly. Brush the edge of the pastry with a little more egg white to seal the spring rolls. Deep-fry in a hot fryer until golden brown. Cut in diagonal lengthways and arrange on serving dishes with the pineapple brûlée and ice cream.

Photograph on page 91.

MARY ROBB

ROCOCO

'I think the way forward is to keep things simple. People like to see the food; nowadays, they don't want anything fancy.'

I'm the kind of person who loves a challenge and loves being busy; I can get really restless if I'm not. Rococo is the place I've wanted to be for a long time. I had worked here before, but left for a while, and then Alan Brown (the proprietor) asked me to come back as head chef.

I've worked in hotels and restaurants since I was sixteen. I've always watched and learned from the people I work with; it's the best way. I worked at Gleddoch House for eight years, and Charlie Price – the head chef there at the time – really inspired me; it was then that I knew I really wanted to cook. After Gleddoch House I came to Glasgow and worked in the Brasserie (prior to the changeover there) and Eurasia; all the time I was learning.

Being able to cope under pressure is a big part of the job, and I'm able to do that. I'm lucky in that Tony Bukhsh who is with me here at Rococo is very hard-working; that makes a big difference. Preparing the menu is also a lot of work, but again I enjoy it.

I'm really interested in flavours; how the dish looks comes last with me. Food does have to look nice, and there is always a lot of work involved in each dish, but I don't believe it has to be elaborate. I think the way forward is to keep things simple. People like to see the food; nowadays, they don't want anything fancy. That's why the menu at Rococo has changed since I've become head chef. The standard and quality of food has not, but the menu has been made simpler. I think our customers have been surprised and pleased with the changes.

I want to stay at Rococo. Eventually, I think I'd like a place of my own, just doing the kind of food I do now but in a smaller restaurant. I know that there can be a lot of headaches involved in running your own place, and that getting established is really hard, but I would like to try.

PIGEON BREAST
WITH BLACK PUDDING, LENTIL GATEAU AND BEETROOT

2 whole pigeons

salt and pepper

1 large courgette

1 aubergine

3 small mixed peppers

100g Puy lentils, soaked in water

25g butter (unsalted)

1 medium-sized onion, finely chopped

2 cloves of garlic, peeled and crushed

olive oil

8 slices black pudding (1.5cm thick)

For the tomato coulis:

450g tomatoes, skinned, chopped and
    deseeded

2 cloves of garlic, chopped

3-4 shallots, chopped

10-12 basil leaves

salt and pepper

For the beetroot dressing:

1 large fresh beetroot

2 tbsp olive oil

1 tbsp vinegar

With a sharp knife, remove the pigeon from the bone and season lightly.

Cut the courgette, aubergine and peppers into small dice.

For the tomato coulis: Sweat the shallots and garlic in a small deep pan with a llittle oil until soft, add tomatoes, reduce by half, add basil. Leave to infuse for 10 minutes. Season and pass through a fine strainer.

For the beetroot dressing: boil beetroot in pan of water until soft (5-10 minutes). Refresh with cold water. Strain, peel skin off and chop. Pass through a strainer. Blend together with oil and vinegar, and season.

Drain and wash lentils. Then add lentils to a pan of salted water and cook till soft but crunchy. Refresh in cold water and strain.

In a pan melt butter and add onions and garlic and cook until soft. Then add peppers, cook for another minute, add courgette then aubergine and cook for 2 minutes. Add lentils, combine with tomato coulis and season. Keep warm.

In a frying pan, fry the pigeon breasts on both sides in a little oil for just a couple ot minutes, then place in a very hot oven for 3-4 minutes.

Grill black pudding on both sides for 2 minutes.

Layer black pudding and vegetable mix on a plate. Place pigeon breast on top and garnish with beetroot dressing.

Photograph on page 99.

PEPPERED DUCK

WITH SEARED VEGETABLES AND CHERRY ESSENCE

For the cherry sauce:

1 tbsp brown sugar

125ml Cassis

2 glasses red wine

1 litre game stock

20 cherries with stones removed

olive oil

3 red and 3 yellow peppers, shaped
   into large squares

3 courgettes, again shaped into squares

12 asparagus spears

4 female duck breasts (trimmed of
   excess fat)

whole black peppercorns (crushed)

For the cherry sauce: melt sugar in the pan. Add alcohol and reduce down a little. Add stock and reduce down until there is a quarter of the liquid left. Season and pass through a fine strainer. Add cherries and keep warm.

Heat a griddle-pan and brush with a little oil. Glaze vegetables and season. Keep warm.

Sprinkle duck breasts with crushed peppercorns.

Pan-fry duck breasts on both sides for a couple of minutes until brown and then roast in a very hot oven for approximately 5 minutes.

Arrange vegetables on a plate. Place the duck on top and pour the sauce over and around.

MONKFISH IN OATMEAL

WITH CARAMELISED SCALLOPS AND CREAMED LEEK PURÉE

For the leek purée:

25g butter

1 medium onion, finely chopped

125ml white wine

1 large leek cut into 5cm pieces, then
   cut into strips, washed

150ml double cream

salt and pepper

carrot, to garnish

potato, to garnish

courgette, to garnish

595g monkfish tails, filleted and
   trimmed

salt and pepper

300g oatmeal

2 tbsp olive oil

50g butter

8 large scallops

juice of ½ lemon

20g spinach leaves, stalks removed and
   chopped

pinch of nutmeg

fresh herbs (e.g. dill and coriander)

For the leek purée: in a deep pan melt butter, add onion and cook until soft. Add leek and cook for another 1 minute, then add white wine. Add cream and reduce until almost thick.

Season and strain, reserving excess liquid. Keep warm.

Prepare the carrot, potato and courgette in solferinos (small scoops). If you don't have this piece of kitchen equipment, cut vegetables into small cubes.

Cook carrot with excess sauce, add potato and at the last minute courgette. Strain and keep vegetables and sauce warm.

Cut monkfish into thick slices, then season and coat in oatmeal.

Heat a little oil in a frying pan and fry monkfish for 2 minutes on each side until brown, adding a little butter at the last minute. Keep warm.

Wipe the pan, add oil and sear scallops for 30 seconds on both sides. Season. Add a little butter and squeeze lemon juice over the scallops until caramelised. Keep warm.

Heat a little butter in a pan, and cook spinach for a couple of minutes until just wilted. Season with nutmeg, salt and pepper.

To serve, place a spoonful of leek on the dish, then place the monkfish on top, then spinach. Finish with the scallops on top. Drizzle excess sauce around and place the herbs on top. Garnish with small vegetables.

MARY ROBB

CHOCOLATE & ORANGE MILLEFEUILLE

(Serves 6)

225g good quality dark
    chocolate

For the orange mousse:

2 sheets of leaf gelatine

2 eggs, separated

50g castor sugar

grated zest and juice of
    2 large oranges

2 tbsp Grand Marnier

300ml double cream,
    whipped

**For the chocolate
mousse:**

2 sheets of leaf gelatine

2 eggs, separated

50g castor sugar

100g dark chocolate,
    melted

2 tbsp brandy

For the fruit coulis:

50g castor sugar

270ml water

150g raspberries

To decorate:

orange zest

fresh fruits

fruit coulis

Melt chocolate and spread thinly over a sheet of baking parchment. When almost set, mark with a small round cutter and chill until set completely. Carefully remove chocolate discs from parchment.

For the orange mousse: soak gelatine in a little cold water for 5 minutes until soft.

Place egg yolks, half the sugar, orange zest and juice in a bowl.

Stand bowl over a pan of hot water and whisk until pale and fluffy.

Squeeze out the gelatine sheets, place in a small bowl with the Grand Marnier and dissolve by standing the bowl in a pan of hot water.

Stir dissolved gelatine and Grand Marnier mixture into egg yolk mixture.

Whisk egg whites with remaining sugar until stiff and then fold in to egg mixture.

Finally fold egg mixture into the whipped cream and chill in fridge until set.

For the chocolate mousse: follow the same procedure as for the chocolate mousse, but whisk the egg yolks and sugar together on their own and fold in the melted chocolate before adding the gelatine, which should be dissolved in the brandy.

For the fruit coulis: make sugar syrup by melting sugar in water. Add fruit and purée. Pass through a fine strainer.

To serve, layer up 4 chocolate discs on each serving plate, piping alternate layers of orange and chocolate mousse between discs, using a piping bag (star nozzle).

Decorate with orange zest, fresh fruits and fruit coulis.

RUPERT & AISLA STANIFORTH

NO. SIXTEEN

'We focus on the main component of the dish, and cook it so well that it doesn't need anything else.'

RUPERT: I left school at sixteen and didn't really know what I wanted to do. I knew I liked and enjoyed cooking, and I was certainly always well fed as a child! So I went to catering college and then started working in hotels. At that point, I was concentrating on having fun, living-in, and having a whale of a time. After more college and exams I started as a commis chef at the Old Vicarage on the outskirts of Sheffield. From there I went to the Marsh Goose in the Cotswolds where I ended up as head chef. It was a really hard, intense three years, but I learned a lot about the business side of things. It was also where I met Aisla. We decided then that, one day, we wanted to open our own business.

AISLA: After working in England, I wanted to come home. Rupert started working in a Glasgow restaurant, and I worked in a call centre in Edinburgh. We have two young kids and had just bought a house in Falkirk when Sixteen came on the market. Apart from the timing, it was ideal. We literally moved in overnight, in December 1998. We thought we knew what hard work was until then: we had pre-booked Christmas parties to deal with – it was right in the middle of the Christmas rush.

RUPERT: Fortunately we inherited Ritchie Blyth, our manager, and the furniture, but otherwise everything else has changed. I cook and Aisla manages front of house, which she loves. We like to keep things fairly simple: we focus on the main component of the dish, and cook it so well that it doesn't need anything else. We try to source the best from our suppliers, and we provide a menu that changes every day, value for money, and a good atmosphere. At least half our clientele are regulars. It's great to get new people in too; they're often sent by our regulars. We will always try to improve on what we are offering.

Our ambition is to reach a position where we can have a bit of time off and see more of our kids. We're doing what we do at No. Sixteen for them really.

HOT LOCAL BEETROOT
IN A CAPER CREAM WITH PARMESAN FRITTERS

500g small beetroot, washed and
  trimmed
500ml vegetable stock
1 tbsp good quality white wine vinegar
a pinch of demerara sugar

250ml whipping cream
30g miniature capers
salt and fresh ground black pepper
60g fresh Parmesan cheese, grated
250g choux pastry

Place beetroot in a large pan of cold water. Bring to the boil and simmer for 1-2 hours. Timing will vary depending on the size and type of beetroot used.

To make the sauce, reduce vegetable stock, vinegar and sugar to a syrup. Add cream. Boil rapidly for 1 minute then take off the heat. Season to taste then mix in capers and put to one side.

Remove beetroot from heat and leave to cool in its own liquid. When cool enough to put your hand in, take a piece of beetroot and rub. The skin and root should come away easily. Cut beetroot into bite-size pieces, if too big to serve whole. Place beetroot in the sauce and return to the boil. Check seasoning and adjust as necessary. Keep warm.

To make the fritters, mix the Parmesan and choux pastry together. Add a pinch of salt. Roll into 12 2cm-balls and deep-fry at 160°C for 6 minutes. Remove and drain on to kitchen paper.

Divide beetroot and caper sauce into four hot serving bowls. Place 3 Parmesan fritters on top of each.

Photograph on page 107.

PAN-FRIED SUPREME OF COD

ON MUSHY PEAS WITH CRISP SMOKED BACON
AND A RED WINE SAUCE

125g dried, split green peas, pre-
   soaked in water for 24 hours
500ml water
a pinch of bicarbonate of soda
250ml good quality red wine
1 litre good quality beef stock
1 tbsp redcurrant jelly

salt and pepper
50g butter, chilled and diced
8 rashers of dry cured, streaky, smoked
   bacon
4 x 135g pin-boned cod supremes with
   skin on and scales removed
vegetable oil

Thoroughly wash and drain split peas. Place in a suitably sized saucepan and cover with 500ml water. Bring to the boil, stirring occasionally. Remove from heat. Add soda carefully, as it will froth up. Return to heat and simmer for approximately 1 hour. Peas should be tender and mushy. Season to taste. Keep warm.

Rapidly reduce 250ml red wine to a syrup. Add beef stock and reduce by approximately three-quarters. Add redcurrant jelly. Season to taste then whisk in all the chilled butter while the sauce is boiling. Keep warm.

Arrange bacon evenly on a baking sheet and grill until crispy.

Season cod on both sides with salt and pepper. Preheat frying pan until it starts to smoke, then add a tiny splash of vegetable oil. Place cod in the pan, skin side down and fry over a medium heat for 3 minutes. Turn over and fry for a further 3 minutes or until cod is cooked. Skin should be crisp and golden brown.

Divide peas on to four hot serving plates. Place cod on top. Pour sauce round the cod and place bacon on top of cod.

BRAISED LAMB SHANK

WITH A GRAIN MUSTARD AND FRESH BREADCRUMB CRUST
AND A GHERKIN HOLLANDAISE

4 lamb shanks (rare leg)

4 tbsp vegetable oil

4 small sprigs of fresh rosemary

16 cloves of garlic, peeled

250ml dry white wine

salt and freshly ground black pepper

1 tbsp Pommery mustard

2 eggs, lightly beaten

6 tbsp fresh breadcrumbs

For the hollandaise sauce:

3 egg yolks

225g melted butter

juice of $1/2$ lemon

salt and white pepper

8 small gherkins, cut into strips

Preheat oven to 190°C (gas mark 5).

Trim any excess bone and sinew from shanks. Fry shanks in vegetable oil until lightly browned all over.

Remove to a deep casserole dish. Add rosemary, garlic and wine. Season with salt and pepper. Cover with tightly fitting lid and cook in the oven until tender (approximately $1^{1}/_{2}$-2 hours). Check halfway through cooking that lamb is not drying out; if it is, add water.

When shanks are cooked, remove from casserole dish. Dry on kitchen towel. Spread mustard evenly over shanks then brush with egg and coat with breadcrumbs. Stand shanks upright in a baking tray and put them back in the oven for 5-10 minutes until golden brown. Serve immediately.

For the hollandaise sauce: over a bowl of hot water, whisk egg yolks with a splash of water until thick. Add melted butter in a thin stream, whisking all the time until sauce has the consistency of mayonnaise. Add lemon juice, salt, pepper and gherkins. Keep warm and serve with shanks.

Serve with boiled new potatoes and green beans.

WARM PEAR AND FRANGIPANE TART

WITH CRÈME FRAICHE

(Serves 8)

For the pastry:

85g butter

32g icing sugar

1 egg yolk

112g plain flour

125g butter, softened

125g castor sugar

2 whole eggs

125g ground almonds

12g soft white flour

2-3 whole pears, peeled, quartered and
   cored

12g demerara sugar (for the glaze)

crème fraiche, to serve

You will need a 12.5cm pastry case

For the pastry: put butter, sugar and egg yolk into a food processor and work together quickly. Blend in flour to a paste. Chill for 1 hour.

Preheat oven to 180ºC (gas mark 4).

Roll out pastry and line tart case. Rest in the fridge for 20 minutes, then bake blind for about 20 minutes. Make sure it is thoroughly cooked and a pale golden colour before removing. Turn oven down to 150ºC (gas mark 2).

To make filling, beat butter and sugar in a food processor until white and fluffy. Add eggs one at a time, allowing mixture to absorb each egg fully before adding the next. Fold in the almonds and flour, ensuring it is thoroughly mixed. Place filling in the pastry case and arrange pears evenly on top. Sprinkle with demerara sugar. Return to the oven for approximately 30 minutes. The tart should be golden brown and spongy to the touch.

Serve warm with a generous portion of crème fraiche.

Photograph on page 111.

MARTIN TEPLITZKY

GROUCHO SAINT JUDES

'At the moment there's a trend for going 'back to basics' with food, and back to the classics too, but I've never left that style of cooking.'

The style of food we serve at Groucho Saint Judes is the style of food I was trained in back in Sydney; I describe it as modern classical. It is classical in that I draw from classical ideas and craft, even though the approach is quite modern.

At the moment there's a trend for going 'back to basics' with food, and back to the classics too, but I've never left that style of cooking. I'm just trying to cook really good food, using great produce and treating it with respect; I'm not trying to prove anything, or be particularly innovative. It's honest food; that's all I care about, that's what stimulates me. I've never followed the fashions. It doesn't appeal to me and I think it displays a lack of knowledge and understanding of what works, and what people want. There was a time when food was so complicated, processed, mucked around with that unless a plate looked like the Hanging Gardens of Babylon, it wasn't considered haute cuisine. That was just rubbish; people don't want that on their plate. An Australian reviewer once wrote that I may have missed a culinary beat, but I deliberately missed a culinary beat! This guy had reviewed me in two different restaurants, a few years apart, and it was a fair enough comment. I like quoting it because it was a conscious decision by me to keep cooking the way I wanted. The fact that things are returning to the basics now shows that I wasn't too far off the mark.

If I want inspiration in cooking, I look up *Larousse Gastronomique*, the classical food and cooking bible. I don't read any contemporary cookery books; I might be missing out, but don't feel like I am. It's been a long time since I have eaten out and come away inspired.

It's been a year since Groucho Saint Judes opened. It's settled down and things are working well. I don't have plans to change the style of food radically in any way, I'm just keen to reach a wider audience.

ROASTED FIGS
WRAPPED IN PARMA HAM WITH GORGONZOLA

8 ripe figs

8 thin slices parma ham

a little olive oil

100g Gorgonzola cheese

150ml double cream

pinch salt/pepper

a small handful of chopped chives

Cut a wee cross on top of figs then wrap in ham. Heat oil in frying pan and seal figs all round until ham starts to crisp up. Place in hot oven (220°C/gas mark 7) for 5 minutes approximately.

Gently melt cheese and cream together in a pan, season. Do not allow to boil.

Add chives to sauce just before serving.

Place sauce on plate and figs on top.

GRILLED SCALLOPS
WITH SQUID INK PASTA, CHILLI AND CORIANDER

24 king scallops

500g squid ink pasta

24 sun blush tomato pieces (50g)

2 red birdseye chilli (remove seeds and
    chop finely)

50ml lime or lemon juice

150ml olive oil

1 bunch of coriander

salt

Grill scallops in a griddle pan or under a grill for 3 minutes each side.

Precook pasta and reheat by dropping it in boiling water for 1 minute.

Drain and place in large bowl.

Add scallops, tomato pieces, chilli, lime juice, olive oil, coriander and a little salt.

Toss all together and serve.

Photograph on page 115.

CRISP ROASTED GRESSINGHAM DUCK
WITH SAUTÉED SPRING GREENS, CASSIS AND BLUEBERRIES

2 medium-size Gressingham ducks
   (other varieties are fine but
   Gressingham is the best)
1 head of spring greens, shredded
salt and pepper
500ml beef stock (reduced to sauce
   consistency)
75ml Cassis
1 punnet fresh blueberries

Season and roast duck on bottom shelf in a hot oven (220°C/gas mark 7) for 1 hour.

Remove and drain off fat; with a sharp knife cut in half and allow to cool.

Return duck to oven and cook for a further $1/2$ hour.

The first cooking brings out a lot of the fat, allowing the second cooking to crisp up the skin.

Remove duck from oven and rest for 5 minutes.

While resting, heat a little of the duck fat in a frying pan and add shredded spring greens.

Season with a little salt and pepper and sauté for a couple of minutes.

In another pan, heat beef stock with Cassis and just before serving add blueberries.

To serve, place greens on plate, cut duck in quarters and place a leg and breast on each plate. Spoon over sauce, dividing berries evenly between plates.

MARTIN TEPLITZKY

RASPBERRY SORBET AND MANGO ICE CREAM BOMBE
WITH WILD BERRY COULIS

For the raspberry sorbet

400g raspberries

125ml sugar syrup (see below)

juice of 1 lemon

For the sugar syrup

150g castor sugar

150ml water

For the mango ice cream

3 large mangoes

300ml crème anglaise

For the crème anglaise

400ml milk

100ml double cream

1 split vanilla pod or 1 tsp vanilla essence

8 egg yolks

150g castor sugar

For the Italian meringue

3 egg whites

175g castor sugar

4 tbs water

For the berry coulis

300g mixed berries (frozen are fine)

100ml sugar syrup

juice of 1 lemon

For the raspberry sorbet: purée raspberries and add sugar syrup and lemon juice. Churn in an ice cream machine or freeze, stirring with a whisk every 10 minutes until frozen. Half fill 200ml pudding moulds with the mixture and return to freezer.

For the sugar syrup: heat sugar and water together until sugar has dissolved.

For the mango ice cream: purée mangoes and add crème anglaise, combining well.

For the crème anglaise: heat milk and cream with vanilla pod or essence. Beat egg yolks and sugar together. Add hot milk and cream to the egg yolks, return to saucepan and stir over a medium heat until thick (about 10 minutes). Churn or freeze as for the raspberry sorbet. Then spoon on top of sorbet, filling pudding moulds to the top. Freeze.

For the Italian meringue: beat egg whites until stiff in an electric mixer. Heat sugar and water together to a temperature of 122-4°C. Add sugar syrup to egg whites slowly, beating continually until mixture is cold (approximately 15 minutes). The meringue should be thick and elastic. Spoon into a piping bag and refrigerate.

For the berry coulis: purée berries, then mix in the sugar syrup and lemon juice. Refrigerate.

To serve, turn out the moulded sorbet and ice cream on to a plate (heating the outside of the mould slightly will help). Pipe meringue around, starting at the bottom and working your way up so as to resemble a beehive. Brown the meringue slightly with a blowtorch or under the grill. Pour the berry coulis around and eat up!

TRACEY THANOPOULOS
& NICOLE CAVES

GRASSROOTS

'Why should people who are vegan or vegetarian expect any less effort to go into their food than others?'

TRACEY: I originally went to art school and did painting, but I'm really glad I ended up in cooking. A lot of the people I've encountered in vegetarian kitchens are art school graduates, and I think that's because it's very experimental and creative. I trained myself as a vegan chef.

We still meet people who are shocked by what we do and what we cook; it's about overcoming stereotypes. Do they think we wear rainbow sweaters and green wellies? Why should people who are vegan or vegetarian expect any less effort to go into their food than others? We've both worked in other restaurants and know the amount of preparation and effort that can go into food there; it shouldn't be any different for vegetarians or vegans. The vegetarian option in a restaurant should not be an afterthought; it's not about a big portion of mush on a plate.

Instead of people referring to this as a vegetarian or vegan restaurant, we want them to refer to it as a great café, whether it's vegan or vegetarian should be of no consequence, because the food's really good. We don't think of ourselves as different with a different customer base – because we're not.

NICOLE: I started at Grassroots in April this year. I'm really interested in vegan and vegetarian food, and working with people with food allergies. I've worked in other restaurants, but it's more of a challenge for me to work here because I constantly have to think about what I'm cooking. Part of the thing that's great about working in a place like this is that everyone's really open to ideas, so you end up learning all the time.

TRACEY: Of the dishes for the menu the soup is one of my favourites. The potato parcels are really tasty, and the baklava is something that people always think is really difficult to make and it's not. And it's good for you!

NICOLE: I'm really into making risotto lately. I've been making it round in the shop for risotto cakes, so this is the risotto before it goes into the cakes. It's so versatile.

THAI WATERCRESS SOUP

1 red onion

3 spring onions

1 yellow pepper

1 tbsp roasted sesame oil (you buy this; warning: it's very strong)

1 tbsp powdered vegetable stock

$\frac{1}{2}$ tsp fresh ginger, finely chopped

$\frac{1}{2}$ red chilli, finely chopped

1 stem of lemon grass, topped and tailed, then cut into two

1 tsp cinnamon

1 tin coconut milk

570ml water

1 bunch of watercress

1 packet of fresh coriander

1 packet of fresh chives

Chop all vegetables finely.

Place red onion in a pan and gently fry in a drizzle of roasted sesame oil. When golden brown, add chopped vegetables except for coriander, fresh chives and watercress. Then add powdered vegetable stock, ginger, chilli, lemon grass and cinnamon. Add coconut milk, bring gently to a simmer and leave for 15-20 minutes. The coconut milk should get thicker. When this happens add water, and bring to the boil. Finally add watercress, half the fresh coriander and fresh chives. Take off the heat when watercress turns an emerald-green colour. This should happen almost immediately. When cooler, drain soup into a sieve. Blend veg in a food processor. Not too much as you don't want a green purée – you want to be able to see the wonderful colours in this soup.

Reheat and serve with the remaining chopped fresh coriander on top.

Note: this soup should be quite thin.

SPICY SWEET POTATO PARCELS

(Serves 4-6)

1 onion

1 red pepper

3 sweet potatoes

1/2 lemon

1 tsp fenugreek leaves

1 tsp madras curry
   powder

1 clove of garlic

1 tsp turmeric

1/2 tsp cinnamon

2 cardamom seeds

1 tsp onion seeds
   (Nigella)

1 tbsp maple syrup

1 tbsp mansun tamari

1 tbsp vegetable ghee

150g red lentils

2 handfuls of fresh

   coriander

1 tin coconut milk

1 packet of Moroccan
   brick filo or ordinary filo

sesame seeds, to garnish

soya margarine, melted

mixed leaves, to serve

Chop all vegetables finely. Remove skin from lemon and slice. Place all of these in a roasting pan along with all spices and flavouring except coconut milk, lentils and fresh coriander. Add ghee. Place in a preheated oven at 200°C. Bake for 50 minutes to 1 hour.

While you are waiting for this to cook, place lentils in 570-845 ml water with a pinch of salt. Cook for 40-50 minutes until lentils have become purée-like.

When roasted vegetables are cooked, remove from oven, add with fresh coriander, coconut milk and lentils to a dish, and mix well.

Using 1 round of brick filo, place filling in the centre of each sheet, fold over either edge and roll away from you. It should resemble a fat cigar. Paint water on top with a pastry brush and sprinkle with sesame seeds.

Note: brick filo comes in rounds and contains dairy products.

Normal filo pastry is usually vegan (check ingredients). Use 2 sheets with this recipe and cut in half lengthways. Paint with melted soya margarine. Fold in the same way. Place on a baking tray and bake in the oven at 180°C (gas mark 4), for around 30 minutes until golden brown. Serve on a bed of mixed leaves along with any type of chutney, chilli jam or raita.

Photograph on page 123.

RISOTTO

WITH GOAT'S CHEESE, ROCKET AND PINE NUTS

1.1 litres stock

2 red onions, finely chopped

2-3 cloves of garlic, crushed

1 leek, finely sliced

I tbsp olive oil

400g arborio rice

350ml white wine (2 glasses)

75g toasted pine nuts

150g goat's cheese

1 handful of roughly chopped rocket

salt and pepper

In one pan, heat stock.

In another pan, fry the onion, garlic and leek with olive oil over a low heat until soft. Add the rice and coat with oil, turn up the heat, stirring constantly, and fry until grains start to become transparent. Add wine. Wait until rice has absorbed all the wine, then start to add stock, 1 ladle at a time. Keep stirring and wait until each ladle of stock is absorbed before adding the next. After around 15 minutes, rice should be cooked: test it. If not, keep adding stock until rice has a slight bite. Once cooked stir in pine nuts and goats cheese. Stir in rocket, and once cheese has melted, check the seasoning and serve.

VEGAN BAKLAVA

(Serves 6-8)

150g soya margarine

350g (total) pistachio nuts, almonds and
   cashews, chopped

150g icing sugar

1 tsp ground cardamom

450g filo pastry

For the syrup

450g sugar

300ml water

2 tbsp rosewater or honey

Melt 50g of soya margarine in a frying pan, add nuts and gently fry. Add icing sugar
and cardamom.

For the syrup: add sugar to water, bring to the boil and allow to simmer for 10
minutes until it becomes syrupy. Finally add rosewater or honey.

Preheat the oven to 160°C.

Grease a rectangular or round tin with margarine. Paint 6 separate sheets of filo
pastry with soya margarine, placing them in the base of the dish. Then place only half
the nut mixture over pastry. Press this down with the back of a spoon. Repeat as
above for next layer, finally laying down 6 sheets of filo on top. Melt remaining 100g
soya margarine. Paint generously over filo. While still uncooked, cut baklava to any
size you want, as you will find the filo very difficult to cut when cooked.

Place in oven and bake for 20 minutes, then turn up heat to 200°C (gas mark 6) and
bake for a remaining 15 minutes. This will allow the filo to become crisp and golden.
When ready, remove from oven and drizzle rosewater syrup over.

It is better to leave baklava overnight, as it doesn't crumble as much. Serve two
pieces as a dish with remainder of syrup, a sprig of mint, and finally dust with icing
sugar. It is also fantastic served with espresso coffee.

Photograph on page 128.

GLASGOW ON A PLATE ② CONTRIBUTORS

CAFÉ GANDOLFI
64 ALBION STREET
GLASGOW
G1 1NY
0141 552 6813

CAFÉ MAO
84 BRUNSWICK STREET
GLASGOW
G1 1ZZ
0141 564 5161

CORINTHIAN
191 INGRAM STREET
GLASGOW
G1 1DA
0141 559 6800

EURASIA
150 ST VINCENT
  STREET
GLASGOW
G2 5NE
0141 204 1150

GAMBA
225A WEST GEORGE
  STREET
GLASGOW
G2 2ND
0141 572 0899

GRASSROOTS CAFÉ
97 ST GEORGES ROAD
GLASGOW
G3 6JA
0141 353 3278

**GROUCHO SAINT
  JUDES**
190 BATH STREET
GLASGOW
G2 4HG
0141 352 8800

LA FIORENTINA
2 PAISLEY ROAD WEST
GLASGOW
G51 1LE
0141 420 1585

LOOP
64 INGRAM STREET
GLASGOW
G1 1EX
0141 572 1472

MALMAISON
278 WEST GEORGE
  STREET
GLASGOW
G2 4LL
0141 572 1001

MOTHER INDIA
28 WESTMINSTER
  TERRACE
GLASGOW
G3 7RU
0141 221 1663

NO. SIXTEEN
16 BYRES ROAD
GLASGOW
G11 5JY
0141 339 2544

**ONE DEVONSHIRE
  GARDENS**
1 DEVONSHIRE
  GARDENS
GLASGOW
G12 0UX
0141 339 2001

PAPINGO
104 BATH STREET
GLASGOW
G2 2EN
0141 332 6678

ROCOCO
202 WEST GEORGE
  STREET
GLASGOW
G2 2NR
0141 221 5004

TWO FAT LADIES
88 DUMBARTON ROAD
GLASGOW
G11 6NX
0141 339 1944

LIST OF RECIPES